I0823039

HOW TO FIND AND KEEP A GAY MAN

PRAISE FOR
HOW TO FIND AND KEEP A GAY MAN

"Hello, darlings–it's me, Mrs. Kasha Davis (a married lady!). And I just celebrated twenty-two years with my love, Mr. Davis. When I dove into *How to Find and Keep a Gay Man*, I was looking for new ways to keep our marriage alive, and what I found instead was a mirror. Both Mr. Davis and I were previously married to women, came out later in life, and had to find self-love first. This book is fun, sassy, and the real deal. It's written like a drag mom talks to her daughter: direct and loving. I heard echoes of our relationship in these pages and couldn't help but connect with its message about self-love as the foundation for any relationship. For me, that meant getting sober; for others, it's about getting real with who you are, what you want, and where you're willing to be flexible. Take the chance. Read the book. Be open and willing to love–and *be* loved. It's worth it!"

—**MRS. KASHA DAVIS**, drag performer and star of *RuPaul's Drag Race* and *Drag Race All Stars*

"This book is a whole damn experience–hilarious, provocative, and wise without ever trying to be. Matt Bays is a delightfully funny and reflective writer, often disarmingly vulnerable, with a tone that immediately puts you at ease. *How to Find and Keep a Gay Man* isn't just another how-to book. It's the most fun I've had getting my ass kicked since that one weird night in Wichita."

—**MATTHEW PAUL TURNER**, *New York Times* bestselling author of *When God Made You*

"Where was this damn book when I was crying in a West Village bar over yet another ghoster who 'wasn't looking for anything serious'—after three dates and a sleepover?! Matt's book is equal parts sass, soul, and sacred gay gospel. As a breakthrough coach and married gay man, I know how much courage it takes to stay out there—vulnerable, messy, and still believing in deep-as-hell love. Matt isn't just giving tips—he's giving truth. The kind that lovingly slaps you across the face and hands you a mirror. Whether you're freshly single, tragically hooked on Grindr, or clinging to a man who won't share his fries—read this. If I'd had this book in my New York City single days, I might've dodged a few disasters (and saved a fortune on therapy). This isn't just a book. It's a survival guide for the gay heart."

—**NANDO RODRIGUEZ**, breakthrough coach, husband, and proud stable gay

"Equal parts wisdom and WTF—this isn't just a dating book. It's a mirror, a megaphone, and a whole damn mood for anyone serious about finding real love. Matt Bays spills the tea, throws some shade, and still manages to serve up real advice that hits where it counts. Whether you're single, partnered, or just figuring it all out, this flirty, fierce, and full-of-heart guide is like your gay best friend in hardcover—ready to tell you the truth and cheer you on every step of the way."

—**STEFAN ARESTIS AND SEBASTIEN CHANEAC**, of the Nomadic Boys travel blog and coauthor of *Out in the World: The Gay Guide to Travelling with Pride*

"Looking for—and holding onto—love doesn't have to be a nightmare. Matt Bays's hilarious, heartfelt, and road-tested tips are all you need to successfully make the journey from hopelessly horny to happy husband."

—**NOAH MICHELSON**, director of HuffPost Personal and cohost of HuffPost's *Am I Doing It Wrong?* podcast

"Matt Bays is a gift, and *How to Find and Keep a Gay Man* is essential reading for any gay single navigating the fierce, fabulous, and often fraught world of modern dating. With practical insights, hilarious anecdotes, and the gentle tone of a trusted friend, this book offers a compassionate guide to building healthier, more fulfilling relationships."

—**BRANDAN ROBERTSON**, author of *Queer & Christian: Reclaiming the Bible, Our Faith, and Our Place at the Table*

ALSO BY MATT BAYS

Leather & Lace: A Gay Man, Lost Love, and a Road Trip with His Dead Sister

Finding God in the Ruins: How God Redeems Pain

HOW TO FIND AND KEEP A GAY MAN

69 SPICY TIPS *for* LASTING LOVE

MATT BAYS

Cover design and illustration by Tim Singleton
Internal design by Jillian Rahn and Laura Boren/Sourcebooks
Internal lettering and illustrations by Tim Singleton
Internal images © Alexey Bezrodny/Getty Images, Anastasia_Stoma/Getty Images, Chorna Olena/Getty Images, Dedraw Studio/Getty Images, Djavan Rodriguez/Getty Images, Eblis/Getty Images, Kenya Aguirre/Getty Images, Liubov Mahda/Getty Images, Ola_s/Getty Images, Pikusisi-Studio/Getty Images, Ramziya Abdrakhmanova/Getty Images, Tenny Teng/Getty Images

Published by Sourcebooks
1935 Brookdale RD, Naperville, IL 60563-2773
(630) 961-3900
sourcebooks.com

Cataloging-in-Publication Data is on file with the Library of Congress.

Printed and bound in the United States of America.
VP 10 9 8 7 6 5 4 3 2 1

To the anonymous man I met at a wedding, still captivated by his wife after many years of marriage.

They were canoodling in a corner when I noticed their sweet connection.
I asked, "How do you keep your relationship this alive and vibrant?"
He replied, "Every morning, I ask myself, *Are you a good person to be married to?*
In my first marriage, I wasn't—so I decided to change that."
She smiled. "And he is. He really is," she said.

It's the best relationship advice I've ever received.

CONTENTS

INTRODUCTION

There is charm school. There are piano lessons. There is curriculum for becoming a podiatrist or administrative assistant. There are even TV shows that teach us how to be drag queens.

Do you have a question?

I do.

Where is the guide to **finding and keeping a gay man**? Because **WE NEED HELP**.

Here's how I know.

A couple of years ago, I posted my wedding video on the socials, celebrating my husband and our love. Having both been married to women for twenty-three years, could it be possible that two newly out gays might have a bit of insight into commitment, sacrifice, and the joy of gay sex? (God, we waited forever.) Or that we might know something about keeping things in a queer relationship fresh, spicy, fun, and meaningful...plus dirty?

While scrolling through the comments on that video, I was shocked by the despair, the deep desire, and the drama from so many gay men who hadn't found "the one." In over a thousand comments, two consistent themes emerged: the desire to **FIND and KEEP a gay man**, and the deep frustration that it hadn't happened for them yet.

There's no way your love is real.

"Soulmates" isn't a thing.

When is it my turn? I'm still waiting.

I had it once, but he cheated on me.

True love is bullshit.

All these messages and more were endlessly repeated by gay men. It wasn't just depressing; it was telling.

My opinion? It's not that hard to find and keep a gay man. But somewhere along the way, **many of us turned into selfish little assholes who don't think of any other asshole besides our own**. And that's not what's going to bring all the boys to the yard.

Think of this gorgeous, flaming, fabulous book as your gay guide to finding and keeping a gay man. It's got sixty-nine entries (because, obviously) packed with bitchy wisdom to get you up to speed. Some are common sense. Some will require a bit of a heart adjustment. And for a few, you'll have to roll up your sleeves and get to work, honey.

Our goal is results, so read them slowly and let them sink in. You might also consider discussing them with your therapist. (So help me, if you don't already have one...) Trust and believe, your therapist knows **it's not as hard to find and keep a gay man as you might think**. They're just waiting for you to figure it out.

Last, if you're rolling your eyes and thinking a book won't cure you, you're right. A book can't. But **YOU** can, which means you'll be playing the role of both patient *and* physician.

I know this might seem difficult, but it's no harder than what you've already been doing, sweetheart. And if you made it through high school algebra, you can do this too. If you didn't, well... I had to take algebra twice. So you're in good company.

ARE YOU READY?

Take a deep breath. Set your ego aside. **And let's do this.**

HOW TO FIND A GAY MAN

I AM NOT GAY, BUT IF I WERE, I WOULD BE THE FIRST ONE RUNNING OUT OF THE CLOSET.

—DOLLY PARTON

PART I

Before You Hit the Bars

Before you bask in the neon glow of your favorite gay bar, let's hit the pause button and prep. Think of this section as your gay boot camp–with fabulous boots, of course. "Before You Hit the Bars" is the crucial soul-searching every gay man must embrace before diving into the dating pool. We'll confront the fears of coming out and dismantle the myth of soulmates, revealing how self-acceptance is the real key to finding true love. Get ready for bitchy wisdom and liberating revelations because **IT HAS BEGUN**! Together, we'll face everything and rise, darling!

01 I'm Afraid to Come Out

Yeah, that'll put a damper on things, Barbie. It sure did for me. This gay dude......stayed in the closet for **WAY** too long.

I can still vividly remember my finger hovering over the publish button on my coming-out post. A handful of people already knew the truth—my sweet momma, a couple of close friends, and most of my family. Because I'd gained some public exposure from my first book, I felt the need to share this part of myself publicly. Not everyone does, and that's okay—it's always about what's best for *you*. For me, revealing this publicly felt necessary, even though I was absolutely terrified.

When I finally shared my truth with the world, everything I had feared came true. Most of the people I *thought* I knew vanished, and my entire life was turned upside down.

Eight years later, I can sum up my feelings about all that I lost in one little hashtag: *#WorthIt*.

Why? Because my fear had never been about *their* homophobia–it was about my own. It was about accepting *myself.*

Without self-acceptance–**without SELF-LOVE**–we can never be the best and brightest version of ourselves. But because I chose to honor myself–because I finally found the courage to come out–**I AM the best and brightest version of myself**. Like I said: *#WorthIt.*

So I say this in love, dumpling: **Get a damn therapist YESTERDAY. Get it sorted.** Because no gay man worth their weight wants to date a guy who's still in the closet. And while you're at it, get that "discreet" hashtag off your dating profile. 😐 Because we're not here to play small. We're not here to hide who we are.

We're here to **LOVE** ourselves.

We're here to be US! 💯

Love you. Mean it.

WITHOUT SELF-ACCEPTANCE—WITHOUT SELF-LOVE—WE CAN NEVER BE THE BEST AND BRIGHTEST VERSION OF OURSELVES.

THE

IS MY

AND HE

LORD SHEPHERD, KNOWS I'M

—TROY PERRY

02 The Soulmate Lie

Liza Minelli says a soulmate is **that one person in nearly eight billion who belongs to you and you alone**.

Awww, that's precious.

Precious bullshit. 

The truth about soulmates? **We DECIDE to be soulmates.**

So, if you're waiting for your soulmate to magically appear, fashioned from the pulsating beat of your favorite gay anthem and the echoes of your broke-ass dreams, don't hold your breath.

When I found my gay guy, we liked each other a lot. Got along great. Sex was amazing. Found each other interesting. We even had that "You complete me" feeling we're all looking for. Oxytocin was coursing through our bits and pieces, and more importantly, we were a good match.

Once we realized we had great chemistry and brought out the best in each other, we made a simple decision: "Let's be soulmates." And now we are. Easy peasy, lemon squeezy.

So, honey, honey, honey...remember this: **A SOULMATE IS SOMEONE WE CHOOSE *and* KEEP CHOOSING, forever and ever, amen**.

It's less mystical. **More logical.** Less romantic. ***More pragmatic.*** With a little dash of magic.

Soulmate divine? Girl, please.

Soulmate, as in, **we love each other enough to cherish one another and put in the work it takes to create our own happily-ever-after**? Yes, sweetheart. Every single day.

Now, grab your latex gloves, because with **fifty million people on Tinder**,[1] finding your soulmate is gonna take a little sifting.

03

Move

Move! As in, relocate. **Because you live on a farm...**or in the middle of nowhere. Seriously, if you've ever said, "Come see my groundhogs down in the holler!" I'm just gonna say it: **Location. Location. Location.**

So there aren't many gays in your neck of the woods. Shotgun Charlie told you he was bi, but turns out that was just a phase.

Here's a good rule of thumb: If you can't get to a JOANN's, a gay bar, or a good gay brunch within thirty minutes, honey...**MOVE**! You don't have to live in San Francisco or Boystown, Chicago. But by god, find a place where your Tinder search yields more than thirteen gays in SpongeBob SquarePants T-shirts. Unless you're looking to land a good ole boy, **get the hell out of there**.

I once knew a gaybie who had hogs. After striking up a friendship, he told me how sad he was that he couldn't find someone in nowheresville. The selection of local gay men on his dating apps was nil. I suggested moving—that there'd be a broader selection in less rural areas. But he wasn't having it. Why? Because he didn't want to leave his hogs.

HOGS. 🤬

I can't. Not even a little bit.

There are TikTok videos of people who think hogs make great house pets. If that's you, fine—just take the hog with you.

Now, I know some of you would say, "Moving isn't financially feasible." Well, I don't buy it. I've done some hard shit in my life, and SO HAVE YOU. Remember this: Your life is **VERY IMPORTANT SHIT.**

Kk?

Figure it out. Load that stinky-ass, motherfucking hog into your fifth wheel **and MOVE**! 🐷 🌽 🚎*

---

* Fast-forward two years. I saw a pic on the socials of the gay boy in this essay. He was standing next to another gay boy at Disney. They were wearing tragic matching T-shirts and Mickey Mouse hats. I'm a nosey mf'r, so I screenshotted the post and texted him, "Who dis?" IT WAS HIS FIANCÉ. Hog heaven. Made me SO HAPPY. Regardless, I said what I said.

04
The Aging Queen

Remember in *Mommie Dearest* when Joan Crawford is examining herself in the mirror, studying her long legs and obsessing over her fading beauty? Her movie career has gone to shit, and the fame she's known for decades is diminishing.

Not long into this dramatic scene, Joan is passionately entangled in the arms of "Uncle Ted." Just as things begin to heat up, Joan's irritation peaks when "little Christina darling" bursts in on her mommy to bring her "a freshener" from the bar. Cut to the next scene and Christina's little ass is being hauled off to boarding school. 😂

Joan wasn't alone in her vanity. I'm vain as hell. **But if we don't balance our FEAR OF AGING with a big fat dose of ACCEPTANCE, we'll never be free of it.** At some point, we must acknowledge there's more to life than being physically desirable.

At fifty-five, I have wrinkles, less hair, and looser skin. The truth is, I'm not getting any younger. **But I'm determined to age**

gracefully. Of course, I want to look my best. But clinging to my youth too tightly? It's a recipe for disaster. Case in point: Babycakes and I saw *The Substance* last night, starring the gorgeously gorgeous Demi Moore. In the movie, Demi's character is in an all-out war against the clock. Spoiler alert–it doesn't go well! Seen it yet? Two words: **earring placement**. By the end of the film, Demi's quest to stay forever young morphs her into a literal monster–a monster that still insists on wearing chandelier earrings to the New Year's Eve bash, yielding... undesirable outcomes (it wasn't pretty).

Listen...

IF YOU'RE A GAY MAN IN YOUR TWENTIES, don't just invest in good skincare. Invest in becoming interesting. **Invest in your heart and soul.** Travel–BEYOND gay cruises. Learn to appreciate art, and not just by decorating your place with naked statues of men. (Why is this a thing?)

Lasting relationships don't hinge on looks—SO HOW ABOUT WE START LIVING LIKE THAT'S TRUE? We're not trying to be Joan Crawford, though we can all agree–her makeup? **Flawless.**

Believe it or not, **being older, more mature, and wiser is a gift,** and if wrinkles and spots come with that gift, sign me up!

I'd rather be a blotchy old man with my beautiful, wrinkled-up husband by my side–**happy, free, and whole**–than an aging queen who never found her true inward beauty.

Now...**BRING ME THE AX!**[1]

THESE ARE NAMES
I SHAN'T FORGET

—Barry —Will & Grace

05 Lower Your Physical Standards

"I'd rather marry ugly and nice than gorgeous and an asshole."

An old gay queen I follow on TikTok said this, and I believe her. None of us is **THAT** cute. I mean, maybe, but whatever. So the question becomes, from a physical standpoint...

What AREN'T you willing to compromise?

Physically, I like a nice face, cuz I'm gonna be looking at it forever. But I don't need my gay man to be stacked. I don't need him to be tall, skinny, or have a head full of hair.

OUTSIDE OF PHYSICAL APPEARANCE is where we establish our **REAL** nonnegotiables. Here's my quick list.

1. A peaceful person
2. Monogamous and enjoys sex

3. Has a job/willing to work
4. Within a decade of my age
5. Able to connect emotionally

Later, we'll clarify how to make your own list of nonnegotiables. But first, notice what *isn't* on mine. I don't care how much money he makes. I don't need him to look like Bradley Cooper. I don't care if he has kids. I don't care if he's spiritual. I don't care if he watches *The Price Is Right* or chews with his mouth open. (I swear, some of you are the pickiest motherfuckers.)

I once dated a guy who smelled like a farm.

His ass, sir, was a disaster. (I just did that.)

Next, there was a guy who was nine inches shorter than me—nicest guy in the world. I bought him a step stool so he could kiss me without craning his neck. True story. He also enjoyed making fun of my age. (Serious age gap... We'll get to that too.)

Personally, **neither of these things were deal-breakers**—not height nor stink. **But it's your list**, and nonnegotiables will be different for everyone.

To make sure you know what you want/need in a partner, ask yourself two questions...

What type of guy complicates my life?

What type of guy ENHANCES my life?

Make a list. Be firm, but fair. (Firm.)

I get that we like what we like, but remember: **What starts cute doesn't always end cute.** "Cute" might be how he finds you. But honey, it's not going to be how he **KEEPS** you. No matter how beautiful he is, **HE MUST BE MORE THAN CUTE**.

So lower your physical standards.

This is all well and good, Matt. But what does this have to do with me? I'm not looking for a cutie. I AM the cutie! What about me?

Great question. Let's talk about you then, shall we? Turn the page, ya little butt pirate. 🏴‍☠️

06

The Stable Gay

A straight guy once told me that two old queens brought him along to the gay bars because he was "eye candy." Yes, honey, he referred to himself as eye candy. He was a circus peanut at best. 🤡

First of all, who told you that you were cute? Also, why are you still telling this story?

So you're cute. Congrats on that. 🎊🍾🥂 A little reminder that "cute" isn't what matters in relationships. At least not to the stable gays. **Because the STABLE GAYS** are on the lookout for a **FULFILLING, LIFELONG LOVE**. I adore a good Latino face. Who doesn't? But if what's behind that face isn't kind or interesting, plan to be...*¡bailando por tu cuenta!* 🎶

On "Fagmalion Part 2," arguably the most epic *Will & Grace* episode **EVER**, Jack McFarland has his "protogay" Barry doing push-ups, which reveals something about the superficial side of gay culture.

BARRY: Are gay guys only about bodies and faces?

JACK: Absolutely not. They're only about bodies. Faces you can cover up with a cute hat or leather hood.

There's nothing wrong with wanting to look our best, but while searching for someone to spend our lives with, **"eye candy" isn't the priority**. How about chemistry? Yep. Sexual chemistry? Uh-huh. **Good pairing?** For sure. (More on good pairing later.) But for **STABLE** gays, **tight pecs, a chiseled jawline, and 🍑 juicy ass 🍑 aren't the main concern**. If these accoutrements come with the man who's best for us, we consider it a bonus. If they don't, it's not a deal-breaker.

TO THE STABLE GAYS AND/OR NON-EYE-CANDIED GAYS: It's perfectly acceptable if these physical traits (pecs, jawline, juicy) are sold separately from what you have to offer. Together, **we stand in our INTERNAL beauty. Cuz stability? Hot AF.** 🔥

TO THE CUTIES: I hate to break it to you, darling, but being cute won't land you a stable gay... Though it might land you a stable **OF** gays.[1] (Get it? Because horses, dumbass. 🐴) Seriously though, **is "cute" really your go-to move for finding a man**? Shaking that ass and serving duck-lip realness? If that's your plan, you probably won't find your **FOREVER** man, because stable gays want **depth and sincerity**. They want someone **interesting and kind**. They're looking for **self-respect, not seduction. Healthy, not hot. Conscientious, not cute.**

STABLE GAYS WANT MORE!

So, if "cute" is all you're serving, here's my two cents: **Spend less time at Sephora and book a damn therapist *AHORA!*** 💃

07

The Cost of Comparison

On January 1, 2017, I was standing on the sidelines at an Indianapolis Colts football game. Confetti and excitement were in the air as I posted live videos of svelte young athletes. On social media, it probably seemed like I had it all—a wife, a family that looked like everyone else's, and sideline tickets to a professional sporting event on New Year's Day. It would've been easy for someone to think, *Must be nice. This guy really has it together.*

But in the locker room of my life, I was a broken closeted gay man. While my outside world projected glam, opportunity, and happiness, **my inside world was crumbling**.

This is how it goes: one scroll, one post, one photo at a time. We compare our average day to someone else's highlight reel and measure our self-worth against the carefully selected snapshots of their life.

At that game, my life was neither better nor worse than anyone else's. How do I know? Because the ups and downs of life are universal.

However, the moment we start measuring our worth by comparing ourselves to others, **we begin to base our sense of *WHAT WE DESERVE* on those comparisons**.

This is the cost of comparison: We undervalue ourselves and settle for less than we deserve in our romantic relationships because we come to believe we're unworthy of someone good, kind, generous, and loving. It's emotional erosion.

If you believe you're unworthy of a good man, the universe will always agree with you. Just know that you're mistaken. You've been duped. You've drawn false conclusions, and my friend, **it's time to let those go**.

Just because someone **HAS** more than you does not mean they **ARE** more—or that they **DESERVE** more. **You deserve it all, superstar.** If there is love within you, you deserve it all. Because **YOU** are one of a kind.

While we may not all have the same wealth, popularity, or opportunities, love is measured equally between us. We just need to find our portion.

But how is that possible? I keep trying to find my portion but continually come up empty-handed.

Rest easy, my love. And keep reading. It's all here.

08
The Asshole Adjustment

Of the things we've discussed thus far, the Asshole Adjustment might just be what saves you—mainly from yourself. If **worthiness, love, and connection** are the symphonies of Carnegie Hall, **the Asshole Adjustment** is the practical work of dragging the instruments into the venue. There's no symphony without the necessary preparations. Well, the Asshole Adjustment is as practical as hell, and **IT IS NECESSARY**.

That said...

Don't be an asshole. And if you know you are, don't see a therapist about finding love—see a therapist about **how to stop being an asshole**. The kind of love you're hoping for isn't possible if you're an asshole, so solve that first, hot stuff.

If you know it's true—that you really are an asshole—don't beat yourself up, but also, don't make light of it by saying things like...

"It's just who I am."

You're an asshole—but you've got your reasons. Once upon a time, something bad happened in your life, and to cope, you turned your pain into sarcasm and meanness. Maybe you built up walls to keep people out. Initially, it seemed to work. But it doesn't anymore. These behavior patterns have left you feeling insecure, broken, and alone. It's time for a change, love. Change is part of the journey.

Change will involve unlearning the behaviors you've relied on—maybe for decades—**to manage life's disappointments**.

Overcoming being an asshole won't be easy, but with the right support, you absolutely **CAN** pull off this level of wizardry. So believe in yourself. Pull a rabbit out of your hat. Wave your magic wand, and start today by deciding, "I will not live my life as an asshole! I want to love someone. And I want them to love me back because **I AM WORTHY OF LOVE**."

Then what?

Sissy that walk to your therapist's office and **dig deep** into what's been fueling your anger all these years.

You can do it, babe. You are *going* to do it.[1]

I like being alone. I have control over my own shit. Therefore, in order to win me over, your PRESENCE has to feel better than my SOLITUDE. You're not competing with another person. You are competing with my comfort zones.

—HORACIO JONES[2]

PART II

Dicks & Dating

Welcome to wild world of “Dicks & Dating.” We’re plunging headlong into the mess and magic of apps and dating. From dodging the relentless barrage of dick pics on Grindr (because instant gratification is a thing of the past, hunty), to knowing how to treat ’em like a lady, we’re going all in. Think of this section as your faithful compass for navigating the highs and lows of modern love, and for better understanding what it takes to be a worthy prospect on the dating scene. Get your swiping finger ready, cuz it’s time to learn the art of sifting through the studs and the duds. The love of your life could be just one swipe away!

09

Get Off Grindr

Let's be honest, getting off...

Feels good.

Lowers stress.

Delivers a more robust immune system (strong like a bull).

Relieves pain.

Plumps lips[1] (Google that shit; true story).

Strengthens pelvic floor (like granite).

There are so many reasons to get off.

Getting off Grindr, however, is a different story.

Are you one of those queens still stuck in the hookup scene while telling your friends and family that you're ready for true love and a meaningful relationship?

If so...**LISTEN UP**!

Grindr is a grind. It isn't the way forward and never was.

Ninety-nine point nine percent of the boys on Grindr? Thirsty. Period, and I mean it.

#DontBeThirsty

This moment of accountability is brought to you by Tinder, Hinge, Bumble, OkCupid, and any dating app without a photo vault.

Perhaps you're thinking, *Please... What does this boy know? He's been gay for ten minutes.* But before writing me off for arriving late to the gay party, just know that two disco balls were delivered to my home yesterday. 🪩🪩

(If that's not fucking street cred, I don't know what is.)

We all know that practically any dating app can be used for hook-ups. However, certain apps (enter Grindr) were **specifically designed** for your naughty bits. And as my little grandma would say when I asked for a second piece of her world-famous pineapple upside-down cake, "Matthew, you've had enough, sweetie."

Grindr got you good and ground. It's time to move on. Time to Marie Kondo that shit: *Thank you, Grindr, but you do not spark joy. You spark naughty boys in harnesses who are too young for me. I dispose of you.* 🚮 *Goodbye.*[2]

For real tho... Get on respectable dating apps and **USE THEM WISELY**. **Because we've got bigger plans for you than that.**

10 Dating Yourself

When I was single, nothing was more annoying than the "Learn to Date Yourself"–type essays I forced myself to read on Salon.com. Those writers can fuck **ALL** the way off.

I'd argue a better definition of "dating yourself" is "**dating someone LIKE yourself**."

Have you ever noticed that when someone's in a relationship with a person they find annoying AF, they start pushing the "opposites attract" theory?

Being attracted to someone is one thing. *Staying attracted is another.*

Let's face it, being in a relationship with a guy who's wildly different from yourself isn't the easiest path. Not that you need to be **EXACTLY** alike—no one wants to see Ed Sheeran and Rupert Grint engagement photos on IG. (Though I am curious what those babies would look like.) But **shared values, common experiences, comparable sex**

drives, and similar ages contribute to compatibility and relational success. And believe it or not, this shit really matters! So...

- If you love a full social calendar, don't get into a relationship with a self-proclaimed homebody.
- If you want monogamy, an open relationship isn't going to do it for you.
- If you're seventy-three, don't date nineteen-year-olds—**NO MATTER HOW CUTE THEY ARE!** That's all I'm saying.

Steer clear of the honeys who live an entirely different lifestyle than you do. They won't complete you—cross my heart, hope to die, stick that needle right up your ass.

Try dating **yourself** instead.

11

When Good Isn't Good Enough

So you've met someone wonderful. He's kind, compassionate, funny, wise, and embodies the kind of inner strength you truly admire. Just remember...**how you feel about him isn't a guarantee of how he will make you feel**. This is a fundamental truth in dating. Even if he's amazing, **it doesn't mean he's amazing FOR YOU**.

It's clear why you're drawn to him—he's a beautiful man inside and out, which can be confusing. But here's what *isn't* confusing: how you feel around him. He may have so many good qualities, **but if being with him makes you feel lonely, anxious, sad, or causes you to question your self-worth, GET OUT**. This doesn't mean there's something wrong with you. And it doesn't mean there's something wrong with him either. It could just mean that **you aren't right for each other romantically**.

No need to label him a narcissist or sociopath to make sense of the disconnect. It's likely just a bad pairing. **Because sometimes good isn't good enough.**

But I love him!

I know. So do I. He's real cute. **But sometimes LOVE isn't enough either.**

Real life example:

Growing up, I never knew where I stood with my very bad stepdad. Even on his good days, I was constantly worried about disappointing him. Every interaction was tinged with a subtle negative energy.

Through therapy, I began to realize which environments were unhealthy for me and learned to avoid romantic relationships that mimicked those same unsettling feelings I had as a kid—even if they were subtle. *This had nothing to do with the guys I was dating* and *everything to do with me*—my past, who I was, and what I needed in a man.

When I met my husband, Chris, I noticed something different right away: There was no anxiety. I could be myself without the confusion or fear of constantly disappointing him. For the first time in a romantic relationship, I felt confident, clear, and entirely myself.

I had dated some really great guys before Chris, but for me, Chris was different. Or to put it more clearly: **I was different with Chris.**

Not every "good" person will be good for you. It's important to understand and accept this reality. We are all shaped by our pasts—by our stories and the choices we've made. The twists and turns we've experienced in life are part of who we are—mind, body, and soul. So we don't just need a good man, darling. We need a man who is good for us. How do we know who that is? **By how we feel around him.**

Last night, Chris and I were walking down the stairs in our little condo. While I was blathering on about how well Kate Winslet has aged, Chris turned to me and, with the sweetest smile on his face, said, "You are just perfect for me. I love you, Matt Bays."

When you find that you are your best self around a good man, pay attention. Take notice. That's when to make your move.

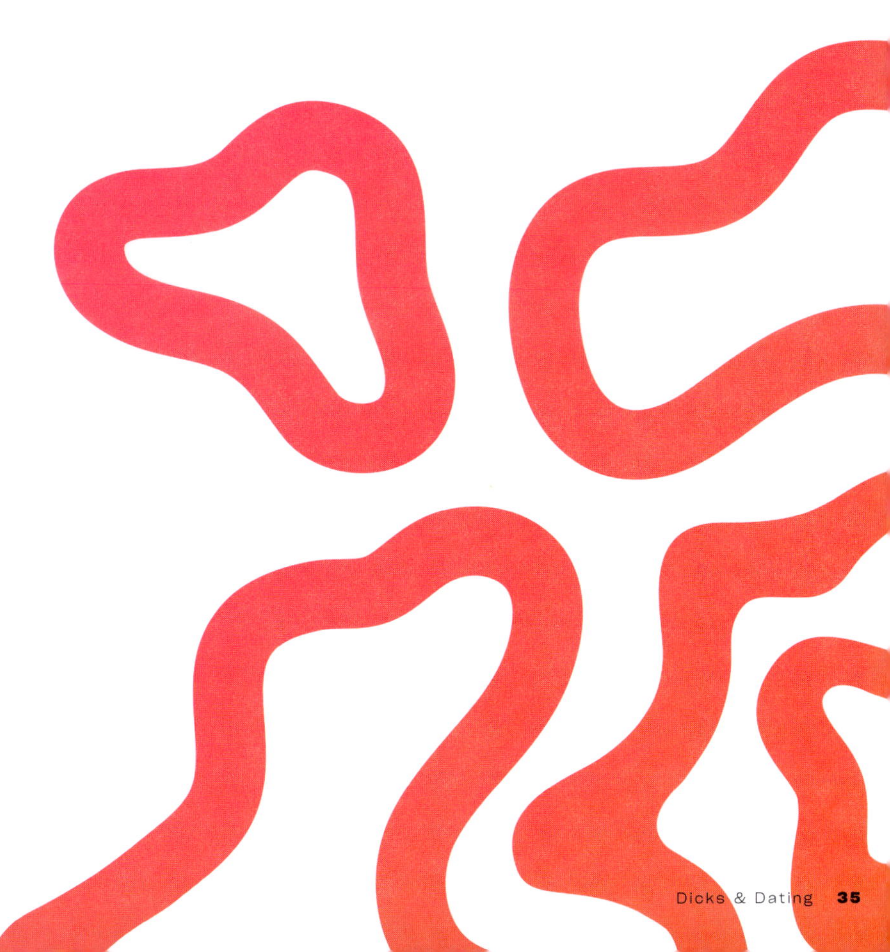

12

The Age Gap Trap

My husband is fifty-seven. I'm fifty-five. In dog years, that's a total of 784. When I first started dating men (at the ripe old age of forty-six), I chose *younger* men. On the low end, my cutoff was thirty. On the high end, thirty-one. Having missed those coming-of-age years, I think I was trying to make up for lost time.

The fabulous Matt Heincker, my cohost on the *How to Find (& Keep) a Gay Man* podcast, loves to give me shit about it. "You were getting them off the school bus, honey!"

Seems I had a type, and I know I'm not alone. Some of you are older than God and still have a cutoff of twenty-five. Dirty birdies. I feel ya.

The issue for me wasn't the age gap, but the disparity in emotional, social, professional, and overall life experience. During disagreements, I often felt more like a father figure offering support than a boyfriend. There were other differences too—like how our career stages made vacation planning difficult, or how I was already thinking about and planning for retirement while it wasn't even on their radar.

The **BIGGEST ISSUE**, however, was that I'd spent years "doing my work," while most of them hadn't reached that point yet. Being with someone while they "do their work," especially when you've already done yours, is like sending your last kid to college and then being handed a newborn to raise.

In short, I struggled to *authentically* connect with the fledglings. I enjoyed and respected them deeply, but the difference in life stages complicated things. After coming to terms with this reality, I decided to find someone who was a hundred. Enter my husband.

That was coldhearted AF. I hope he takes it out on me later. 

Maybe it's time to stop chasing the young'uns, because we all know that the young guys don't stick around. And **IF** by some miracle they **DO** stick around, there's a good chance it'll be because you're taking care of them. **And we're not here for day care.**

I hate to sound like the closed-minded gay who says, "Find someone your own age," but it's pretty clear that while pursuing younger men (or older, if you're a daddy chaser) might help you *find* someone, it won't necessarily help you *keep* them. Is it possible that relationships with a substantial age gap will be satisfying? Of course, but only because anything is possible. Statistically speaking, it isn't likely.

Fuck you, Matt Bays!

I know. It's annoying. But also true.

I date younger guys because it doesn’t require as much commitment and I have complete control over them.

—ANONYMOUS[1]

THE ULTIMATE GUIDE TO CRAFTING YOUR DATING APP PROFILE

Hey gorgeous, let's get digital!

Creating the perfect dating app profile is important, so grab your laptop, and let's dive into making a profile that screams YOU!

1. START WITH PICS

Your Profile Pic: Choose a photo that pops. Keep it casual and fun. A genuine smile is best—let them see your face first. DO NOT LEAD with a shot of your abs, ass, or shirt unbuttoned all the way down to your flowers. It's fine to show off your body, just keep it appropriate, and place it toward the back of the pile. You're looking to find a good guy. Leading with an erotic body shot is thirsty, and we're above that.

Show Them Your Passions: Are you a pet lover? Show them that little cutie. What about your travels? Definitely. Also, pics of yourself with friends or family lets them know it's not all about you, so keep the glamour shots to a minimum.

No-No Pics: Be aware of what's in the background of your pictures. No one wants to see your dirty apartment or bathroom. No tacky mirror selfies with your tongue hanging out. Halloween costumes? Only if it's October.

Keep your photos cute and lighthearted. You might want to consider asking a friend for help. My creative friend Beth helped curate a few great shots for me. Remember, while you might love that very hot pic of yourself with the killer smize, pics like that can be intimidating or even considered egotistical. Let them see YOU, not a fantasy.

2. MAKE MAGIC WITH YOUR BIO

Be You, Unapologetically: Be honest, be bright, be bold. Share what makes you tick. Whether you're a gym bunny, a gaming nerd, or a night owl, the right guys will appreciate the real you. Consider including a life quote, as long as it's not, "LET THE HUNGER GAMES BEGIN!"

A Dash of Mystery: Don't spill ALL the tea. Leave space for curiosity and conversation.

3. A SPOONFUL OF HUMOR

Laugh, Honey: Wit is effective. A clever quip or joke can make your profile stand out from the others. Don't take yourself too seriously. A dating profile isn't the place for a detailed account of your last breakup, or to mention that your ex lives in your basement. Keep things light.

4. WHAT'S YOUR FLAVOR?

Likes and Dislikes: Don't specify whether you're a top, a bottom, or verse. You're not ordering food. If you treat dating apps like a menu, it's going to feel transactional. Besides, if the sexual chemistry isn't there, you could end up with a new friend. Also, share the things you love: movies, working out, weekend getaways, junk food, great books, drag brunch. And the things that are deal-breakers for you: smokers, heavy partiers, homebodies, open relationships, monogamy. Let them know. This will help filter out guys that aren't for you.

5. UPDATE REGULARLY

Keep It Fresh: Update your profile seasonally or with your latest obsessions. An evolving profile keeps them interested and KEEPS YOUR PICS CURRENT. Do NOT post photos of what you used to look like. You're beautiful now. Be honest. Keep it real.

6. ONCE THEY'VE SWIPED RIGHT...

Flirt a Little: Ask questions about their profile: "I saw you have two sons. What's being a dad like?" Or react to one of their photos: "You have great style. The shirt in your third pic...LOVE." End with something flirty that invites a message. "Great pic of you and your friends in that quaint little bistro. Let me know if you're up for a coffee date... I'm buying." 😊 And God help us all, do not start your first DM with "Hey." 💀

You are setting the stage for your love story. That said, the goal isn't to attract any guy—it's to reel in *the* guy! The one who's going to love you for you. So, put your most authentic self out there. The rest? It's just a matter of time.

Love you. Mean it. 💖

13

Dick Pics

I was faithfully married to a woman for twenty-three years. So when it came time for this baby gay to start dating, it had been a while.

When I first signed up for the dating app SCRUFF, I had no idea what a "private album" was. Naively, I took the bait, expecting pictures of dogs. Yeesh. Hot dogs instead, hold the panties. And the angles you boys are working with those iPhones... WOWZA.

Call me crazy, but I didn't lock down a single date with a guy who sent me his private album. Not one. Why? Because I knew it wasn't going to lead to the kind of relationship I was seeking.

Let's be real: **if you're leading with Cocky McOne-Eye, you've already told me all I need to know**. I'm not saying be a monk, but maybe put away your junk. 🤓

I once matched with a guy on SCRUFF and was interested in getting to know him—right up until he sent several unsolicited photos of his...gentlemen sausage. I messaged back and told him I was no longer interested. A few days later, I was at Warby Parker getting my glasses adjusted. Guess who worked there? Yep–Mr. Sausage.

It was awkward having him wait on me when *HE* knew that *I* knew exactly what his knob looked like...in his bedroom, his living room, and on his balcony. People are always saying, "If you get nervous, picture them in their underwear." Okay. Or just naked.

Part of me wanted to be honest and say, "Dude, I was actually looking forward to getting to know you, but I'd never be able to trust a guy who sends unsolicited dick pics to a person they've never even spoken to."

Moral of the story: Maybe you HAVE not because you BEHAVE not.

Personally, I wanted more. What about you, boo? Want something real? Want your forever man? Because we deserve someone who will be with us through **THICK** and/or **thin**. If that's what you want, too, change it up, babycakes.

Show them your heart. Not your part.

MY SEXUAL ORIENTATION POINTS TO NOTHING MORE THAN MY LOVE FOR ONE MAN, YOU.

—MICHELE MELEEN

14

Dating: Are You Good at It?

I once had a dinner date that felt like a twelve-hour shift at Casual Corner. He barely spoke. I asked question after question, leaving long awkward pauses, giving him plenty of time to ask about my pink leather Pumas. Nothing. Fifteen minutes in, I knew we weren't a match. I decided to use the rest of our time together as date practice.

"Tell me about your family. What do you do for a living? What was coming out like for you? In your profile pics, you're serving Karamo Brown, but in person, Steve Harvey. What's that about?"

When the bill came, he didn't even *pretend* to pat his empty pockets to split it. He was nice enough, but it was clear **he didn't know the first thing about dating etiquette**. I mean, *answer* a damn question, then *ask* a damn question.

A good friend once told me about a date he had with a gorgeous Marvel-esque guy—the likes of Aquaman. From across their bistro table, the first thing Aquaman said to him was, "Is your butt hungry?"

IS YOUR BUTT HUNGRY?

God help everyone. God help the starving children. God help the old lady I saw driving a hot pink Fiero. And God help us gays—pretty please with sugar.

"¿Tu trasero tiene hambre?"

Even in Spanish it's awful. And I am dead. **DEAD** I tell you.

Remember...it all begins on that first date, and on a **GOOD** first date, a guy should engage you respectfully. Same goes for you. Ask about his life and be genuinely interested if he shares his story. Offer to split the bill when it arrives. And if you're seeking a man for the long haul, don't make every date a hookup.

TAKE THINGS SLOW.

Treat 'em like a lady. Don't be an asshole. Learn how to play the long game.

15

Wingman

When it comes to dating apps, the words "I give up!" could simply mean, **"I'm sick of trying to find someone who will love me. It's never going to happen. I've tried EVERYTHING!"**

This sort of response isn't about fatalism, it's about fatigue.

Anyone who's spent time on the apps has felt this way. You match with someone and never hear from them again. Or everything seems to be going well; then you're ghosted. Or you show up for a first date only to realize the guy used photos from 1996 and, in real life, looks like a potato. (And not a cute potato.)

After a while, it's easy to lose sight of your goal of finding love–to give in to the fuckery of dating apps and compromise your values for shallow experiences that won't bring you closer to a meaningful relationship. Or you might just delete the apps and stop dating altogether.

Truth: IT'S NOT EASY.

More truth: BUILD A BRIDGE AND GET THE FUCK OVER IT.

You can always throw in the towel, draw the blinds, and watch Sasha Colby take the crown while feeding yourself string cheese and baby carrots. Or you can put on your big boy panties and **MOVE TF FORWARD**.

You need a wingman. Or a wing hag. Or a wing team. Ultimately, you need someone who will celebrate your successes and offer perspective during your breakups.

Story time!

While I was out in these streets shopping for a man, my wingman, Matt Heincker, kept me sane. He pushed me to go on dates I didn't want to go on and made me break up with guys we both knew weren't right for me. We laughed together at my dating horror stories, and most importantly, he single-handedly discovered my husband.

One evening, while sitting on a purple pouf in his living room, Heincker scrolled through the Tinder options on my phone. He stopped on Chris, turned the phone to me, and said, "What about him? He's gorgeous. He's a family man. And his bio is articulate and delightful."

My only response? "He looks like a game show host."

Thankfully, Heincker was over my bullshit, and without my permission, swiped right on Christopher David Evans. *It's a match!* flashed across the screen, and two weeks later, I was in bed with my future husband. 💘

Listen...it's **CRUCIAL** to have a companion on this journey. Someone we can talk to about the guy who smelled terrible down there. 😷 Someone to share those outrageous app messages or the photos of that guy on a horse wielding a tomahawk with. (True story. Happened to a friend of mine.) 🪓 👷 🦄

Having a wingman who will listen, provide feedback, and laugh with you through the madness makes the whole experience less daunting. Believe it or not, it **IS** possible to enjoy the bizarre, terrible, wonderful, gruesome, lonely, mind-numbing, and earth-shattering experience of twenty-first-century dating.

So get a wingman. And hang in there, cupcake. 🧁 💖 No one should be doing this alone.

SEES A RED FLAG

LET ME GET SOME SCISSORS. I CAN MAKE A HEART OUT OF IT.

—ANONYMOUS

16

Red Flags & Green Lights

Every damn time you see a red flag, GUUURL, you grab your scissors. Why? Because you're convinced you can turn that red flag into a red heart. Little snip here, little lie to yourself there, and voila—you've made that disaster of a man your boo.

Question: Are you looking for a LOVE story or a LIFE story?[1]

A love story doesn't require anything other than *your* body and someone else's body. **A LIFE story**, on the other hand, requires more than love.

Like what?

Like compromise. Like ambition. Like empathy, negotiation, and chemistry.

A love story is passion, excitement, and typically short-lived.

A **LIFE** story is building something with another human being. Finding alignment in your core values. Sticking together through tough times. Growing old with a man you've loved for decades.

Red flags aren't just the personality flaws. When it comes to finding and keeping a gay man, red flags are any characteristics we don't value in a romantic relationship—particularly those behaviors that indicate he isn't looking for something long-term.

What about green lights?

Green lights are the qualities in eligible men that attract you **in HEALTHY ways**—like kindness, humor, a love for travel (if you love to travel), a love for animals (if you love animals), patience, joy, peace, or ambition (if these things matter to you). **MOST IMPORTANTLY**, it's the mutual desire to build a life together the way Christopher Reeve wanted to build a life with Dr. Quinn, Medicine Woman, in *Somewhere in Time*.

I'm gonna level with you. Little baby Jesus knows exactly what you've been up to on the apps, in your bed, cruising the park, and in the stall of that filthy restroom at the club. If you say you want a LIFE story, prove it.

How?

TAKE DATING SERIOUSLY.

Hookup boys who are clearly not interested in a life story: **BIG RED FLAG**.

Green lights keep you moving forward. So if you want a relationship that will go the distance, **LOOK FOR THE GREEN LIGHTS**.

Visualize them. Can you see them out in front of you? Because I can. Your sweet momma can. **All your friends can.** But it's not up to us, love. You must find them for yourself.

And when you see one, if that sumbitch turns yellow, put the pedal to the metal and **FLOOR IT**!

Floor it for a love story?

No, no, no, Little Debbie. **Floor it for a LIFE story!**

17 If What You're Doing Isn't Working…

You've been searching for love in all the usual places—bars and apps. While I'm a huge fan of using the apps effectively, at some point, you must ask yourself, *Am I making progress?*

Meaning: Are you meeting guys who are relationship material, or are you just repeating the same old patterns and expecting different results?

IF WHAT YOU'RE DOING ISN'T WORKING, TRY SOMETHING ELSE.

If you've turned down invitations from friends who want to set you up, how about going instead? Even if it doesn't work out, it could light a fire under your ass for the cause. Ever considered volunteer work with an LGBTQIA+ organization in town? There are men there—good, helpful, hot men. **And if they're volunteering**, they're probably a different breed than you're gonna find on Grindr. So grab your purse and get going, Anita Fella.

I recently saw a gay guy on TikTok bitching about Colton Underwood. He was pissed that Colton came out and was engaged to a hot daddy in about fifteen minutes. Dude was **FRUSTRATED**–said he's been searching for love for twenty-seven years and still hasn't found "the one." He was good-looking and articulate, so I had to wonder, *Is he mean? Difficult? What's keeping him stuck? Fear? Assholery? Emotional immaturity?*

He told his followers that he deserved something he wasn't getting, suggesting that LIFE was against him. **But the universe isn't against us.** A more helpful approach would be to ask the question...

"What am I doing wrong?"

This is the part of the movie where the bestie makes empty declarations: **"You're not doing ANYTHING wrong. You're such a good person. It's just bad timing."** 😑

She's a good egg, for sure–we all need someone like that in our lives. **Just don't listen to her, k?** Because her well-meaning attempts to ease your pain by insisting that your struggles to find a man have nothing to do with you will only keep you stuck. What I'm saying is, **if it's been twenty-seven years, you absolutely ARE doing something wrong, hot dog**.

Maybe it's time to own it. **Maybe it's time to try something else.**

Because what you're doing isn't working, henny.

So...

Get nice. Get some honest friends. Get new ideas for meeting men.

GET MOVING.

LIVES IN MOM'S BASEMENT
CATFISH CONNOR
TRUE LOVE
ASSHOLES
EMOTIONALLY UNAVAILABLE

IF YOU CAN'T
LOVE
YOURSELF,
HOW IN THE
HELL
YOU GONNA
LOVE SOMEBODY
ELSE?

—Mama RU

PART III

The Best Boyfriend You Can Be

Alright, darlings! It's time to get your hands dirty because this section isn't fucking around. You wanna be the partner you always dreamed you could be? Well, it's gonna sting a little, because transformation is painful, ya heard? This isn't just advice—it's a heartfelt challenge to lift up, lean in, and love hard. We're battling a few inner demons while learning to genuinely celebrate everything—yes, everything—that makes your partner the fabulous person they are. This is where mutual growth becomes profound commitment. We're turning the love up to eleven!

18 Unwild & Waiting

When I came out, I had several friends tell me I needed to let my hair down and figure out who I was—to sow my wild oats. To find my place in the gay community by kicking the tires, clubbing, and getting a little wild.

But I didn't want to do that. I already knew who I was—a dad, someone who treasured friendships, a creative person, an empath. I didn't need to do things differently just to fit in. Some people might genuinely need that experience, which is great, **but it wasn't for me**.

Instead, I stayed true to myself. I dated one person at a time, was honest, returned phone calls and texts, didn't ghost guys I matched with, respected myself and others, and had conversations I could be proud of. My DMs were rated PG at best. **I didn't compromise my values, and I didn't complicate the process.** I did what felt natural.

This was me.

Back in those days, the constant refrain in my head was, *Love knows you're out here, Matt. It's coming for you. It will show up. Just stay the course. Keep being you and wait for it.*

So I did. I waited for it—**unwild and waiting**.

Well, guess what? On my fiftieth birthday, **HE showed up**—handsome and wonderful and perfect (for me).

I still believe we choose to be soulmates by treating each other well every single day. When you show your boo **respect, kindness, and love**, it makes you feel like soulmates—which, in my opinion, **is what MAKES you soulmates**.

In the dedication of this book, you might've noticed I mentioned a man who once told me...

"Every morning, I ask myself, 'Are you a good person to be married to?'"

READ THAT AGAIN, and this time SAY IT OUT LOUD.

I'm not kidding when I say...**THIS IS THE BEST RELATIONSHIP ADVICE I'VE EVER RECEIVED**.

(It's so simple.)

My job is to show up in love every damn day. I absolutely **DO NOT** take Christopher for granted. We are a gift to each other—**something we're BOTH very mindful of**. It's why we celebrate our love and our life together as often as possible.

We are two lucky boys. 🍀 **And we treat each other like two lucky boys.**

I waited fifty years for my man. **Fifty!** It wasn't easy, but he was worth the wait.

So fucking worth it. 😊

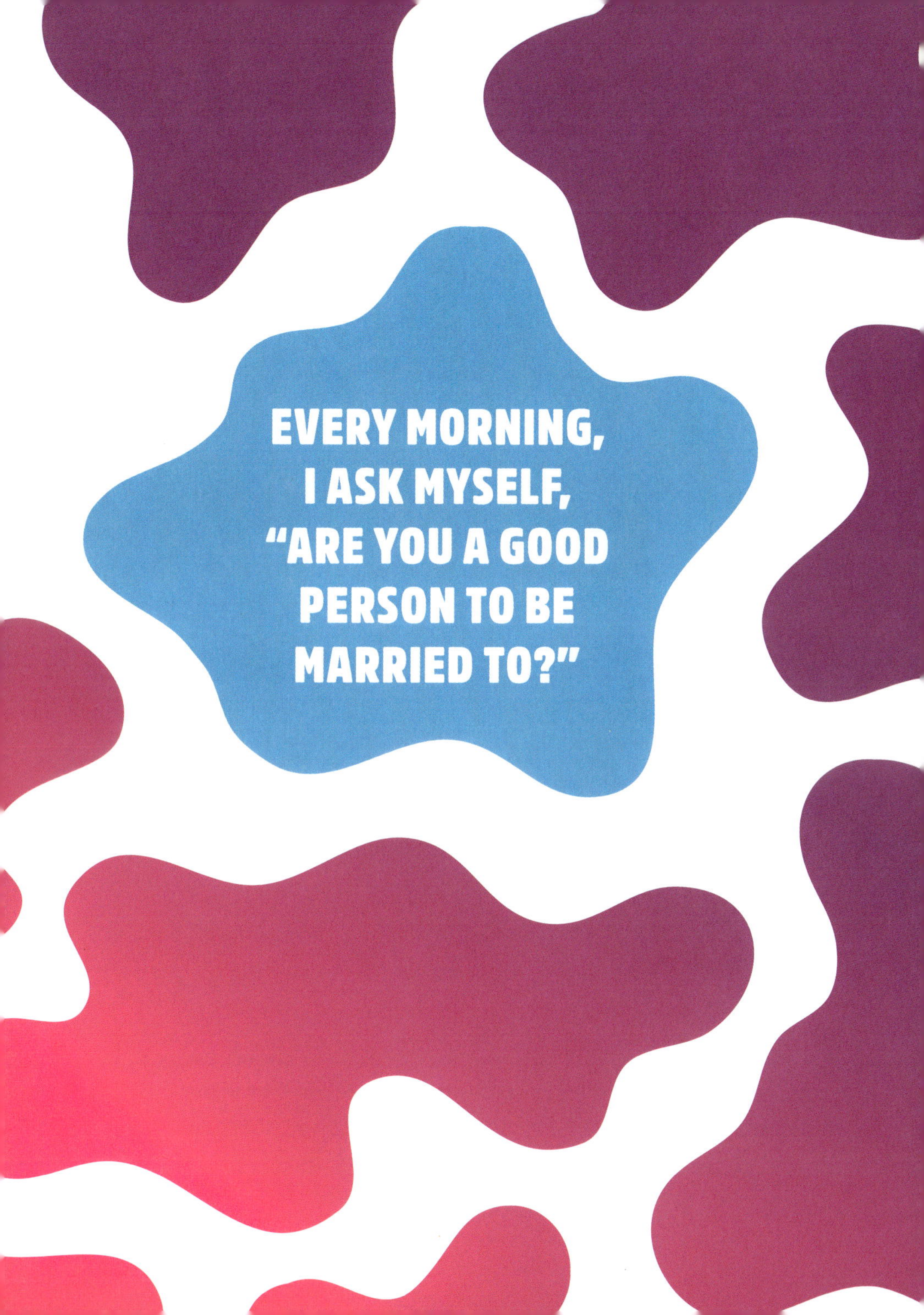
EVERY MORNING,
I ASK MYSELF,
"ARE YOU A GOOD
PERSON TO BE
MARRIED TO?"

19

God, Gay... Good Lord!

I once worked for very large conservative churches (you know the kind). Apparently, they weren't super into me coming out, 😬 while I wasn't super into them not wanting me to come out. A beautiful win-win, **and they can kiss my gay ass.** 😚

On social media, I eventually had to ask people to unfollow or unfriend me if they weren't supportive of LGBTQIA+ rights. Some were outraged. **I searched my pants pockets but couldn't find one fragile fuck to give.** A very religious man commented about Jesus-this-and-that. He seemed quite sad that I was gay. No worries, though. The doctors say he's going to be fine...tubes up his nose and whatnot.

What exactly does this have to do with finding and keeping a gay man? A lot, actually. Especially since **68 percent of Americans identify as Christian,**[1] **and 33 percent of religiously affiliated LGBTQIA+ folks STILL haven't reconciled their religious beliefs with their sexuality.**[2]

If I could, **I'd absolve every last one of you who is still struggling with whether or not God cares if you're gay**. Listen to me: She ain't mad–I asked her. **She's gloriously giddy about it and spinning her Liberace records as we speak.** Take it from this ex-pastor who's queer as a football bat: **YOU ARE GOOD WITH GOD**. Cross my heart, hope to never die.

It's time to make peace with this issue, lest it impact our ability to **love freely** or **have sex without shame**. Because how we feel about ourselves **WILL IMPACT OUR RELATIONSHIPS**. And if there's one thing we've learned from the **incomparable RuPaul...**

"If you can't love yourself, how in the hell you gonna love somebody else?"[3]

True damn story.

GOD LOVES YOU. And so do I.

So get well soon, angel. Because **you're good with God**. She hasn't lost a wink of sleep over you. **She is PROFOUNDLY proud of you.** Kisses, kisses, kisses all around. 😘

20
Don't Be a Player

His profile pic was a mashup of Colin Farrell and George Clooney. In real life, he was more CeeLo Green and Harvey Fierstein–only not as cute.

We exchanged a few messages on SCRUFF before deciding to FaceTime. When he appeared on-screen, he was smoking one of those extra-long cigarettes.

Girl! What was he wearing?

I'm glad you asked. (Rubs hands together.) This queen was serving Betty Grable realness in a leopard-print silk robe with a fur collar. It was everything! Apart from sitting in a garage with a blue plastic kiddie pool hanging on the wall behind him, he was giving OG Eleganza, honey.

"So..." he began while lounging in a lawn chair, "are you a top or bottom?" 👀 A plume of smoke billowed from his mouth.

"Oh," I said, caught off guard. "I'm not interested in talking about that."

He giggled. "God, you're gorgeous. What about fetishes? Are you into fetishes?"

"Well..." I stammered. "I don't know...ummm." I took a deep breath.

"I mean, how do you like it? You are SO HOT. Do you know what I would do to you?" He shifted seductively...**IN HIS GODDAMN LAWN CHAIR**!

I whispered a prayer.

God, deliver me from CeeLo Fierstein. I swear I'll never ask for another thing.

Several minutes into our FaceTime, I told him I wouldn't be joining him that night...or ever.

As soon as those words left my mouth, the screen went black.

He wanted a hookup, which is fine for consenting adults. But if you're pursuing **SERIOUS love**... No, baby. Just no. Even if he'd been a mashup of Christian Bale and Timothée Chalamet, there was no alignment between us. Therefore, not worth it. (Did I mention the lawn chair?)

Here's the gay gist: If this—even in a small way—is how you act in romantic encounters, stop it. **EVERYONE thanks you.** Transactional interactions are beneath you. Lead with good manners. Stick to your values, keep doing the next right thing, and wait for it.

Remember: We're not here for a quickie. We're here for a longie. (Oh, shut up.) 🙄

21

Keep It Simple

A friend of mine had been dating a guy for several months and was growing increasingly frustrated by his inability to commit or even define their relationship. Was it casual, serious, or simply transactional? After being strung along in this on-again, off-again dynamic, my friend reached out for help.

"I don't get it, Matt. First, he says he's interested; then he says he's not, but still enjoys being around me. Now he's changed his mind **AGAIN** and wants to date but doesn't want to be exclusive. Also, he keeps asking me for advice about his other dating relationships. **I'M SO CONFUSED."**

"I'm so confused!" Best damn thing I heard him say.

Finding a gay man is complicated enough. Dating doesn't have to be. So keep it simple: **If a person is making you crazy now, they will ALWAYS make you crazy.** So split, kitten—say goodbye. It just means they're not right for you. Some gay guys are into this sort of game playing. (I wasn't.) They like the drama. (I hated it.)

Them: But he's cute.

Me: It'll wear off.

Them: His ass tho...

Me: He's an ass tho.

Them: He's a good guy.

Me: Please. He's a child who doesn't know what he wants. How long must we keep having this conversation?

If two complicated people want to partner up and complicate the world together, great. Sounds tedious. **But we're not here for mind games.** This isn't our romantic dream. **We aren't here to be confused, passively aggressed, or strung along.** We must stop thinking that this sort of fucked-up experience is our only option. **IT ISN'T.**

Find someone who is AVAILABLE. If they aren't, or if they're waffling on how they feel about you, **move it along**. 🏃 And I mean move it **THE FUCK** along before you get sucked into their cuteness and lose three years of your life. ⌛

Available? Yes. Unavailable or unwilling to clearly articulate their availability? Say it with me... **NO**!

Keep it simple.

22
Fear—Part 1

Remember when we spoke about the Asshole Adjustment? I'm gonna save you a little time. **Being an asshole is about fear.**

Every diva on *Drag Race* who'd rather shift a sister's wig than resolve a disagreement like an adult; every caustic exchange you've seen in the comment section on IG, TikTok, or Facebook; the gay guy who feels powerful each time he "ruins" someone with his wit or verbal dexterity—all of these are fueled by one thing: **FEAR**.

They're not angry—**they're afraid**.

And just as an FYI...99 percent of the time, *fear is about something we're trying to protect.*

Like what?

Here are a few options to get you started. Take your pick: fear of rejection, fear of abandonment, fear of intimacy, fear of being taken advantage of, fear of losing independence, fear of not being enough, fear of change.

Any questions?

As gay boys, **we've been through a lot of shit**. And often, instead of being vulnerable and talking about our hurts, we turn to anger because in the short term, it's easier.

I had a good friend once tell me, "Anger is secondary emotion," which is why we're no longer friends. 🙃 She's right though: *Anger is a side effect. Fear is the disease.*

Most of our struggles in life are about fear. Period. Full stop. Final answer.

So in your next therapy session, start with the fear and stay there. Don't waste time refereeing symptoms. Get to the root cause of your bad behavior. Deal with what's *really* sabotaging your dream of finding and keeping a gay man.

Deal with the fear.

But how?

Turn the page, kitten.

MY "FEAR" IS MY SUBSTANCE AND PROBABLY THE BEST PART OF ME.

—FRANZ KAFKA

23

Fear—Part 2

Once you understand that fear is keeping you stuck, you're ready to move forward.

Great. So what do I do?

Before we go any further, stop and take a deep breath. Lay this perfect little book on your lap, close your eyes, and breathe for thirty seconds–in through your nose, out through your mouth. 🧘

Did you do it? Let's move on.

You've been searching for the silver-bullet solution to your fear for quite a while, but there isn't one. There is, however, a remedy. But before I say more, I need you to lower your expectations.

I'm sorry, what?

You heard me–lower your expectations. This step is crucial because **expectations are premeditated resentments**. (Write that down.)

Have you lowered them? Are you expecting nothing? Perfect. Because that's exactly what you do: **NOTHING**.

Not a goddamned thing.

Something happens to you now, and you have nothing to do with it.

Fear is about controlling outcomes, which has never worked for you. It's time to try something else, **which is nothing**.

I realize this feels like some sort of riddle. It's not. It's a different mindset, which is going to take time to get your head around.

Listen, you are never going to stop being afraid—ever. And that's okay. Because fear isn't the issue. **Being AFRAID of the fear—THAT'S the issue.** That's what is keeping you stuck.

And the remedy?

Stop being afraid of fear.

How?

By accepting that fear isn't the enemy. In fact, **the universe has a purpose for it**. Crazy, right? The only thing you need to "do" is **give the universe access to your fear, so it can help identify the obstacles in your life and guide you to a better place**. What I'm saying is: instead of fighting against it, get curious about it.

When you're afraid, ask yourself:

What is my fear trying to tell me?

What does it want me to avoid, explore, or be excited about?

Accepting fear as a natural part of life will keep you from feeling emotionally paralyzed each time it shows up. Reacting with agitation or anger **often leads to nasty breakups, neediness, ego problems, or low self-esteem**. That said, **let it be**. Let the fear wash over you. Because once we stop battling it, we can begin addressing the real issues that are holding us back.

Most of us were taught to see fear as a warning—a signal that something terrible is about to happen. But when we shift the lens and allow it to guide us instead, we create safe, nonjudgmental spaces for self-reflection, growth, and healing.

SOMETIMES, THE HARDEST PART ISN'T LETTING GO, BUT RATHER LEARNING TO START OVER.

—Nicole Sobon

PART IV

Breakups

Breakups. We've all been there—sobbing in our cars to our favorite sad-ass playlist, wondering if we should give that old relationship another shot, looking for the nonnegotiables list we tossed out the window for love. Here's the deal: breakups aren't just about endings; they're about beginnings. They're about finding the strength to say no to what's not working. In this section, we won't sugarcoat the pain—no, honey, we'll face it head-on and learn to let go of whatever is no longer serving us. Is it complicated and stupid and awful? Of course it is. But remember, what doesn't kill you can fuck right off. We're breaking up with the past to make room for the future, because that's where your true love is waiting for you.

24

Breaking Up 💔

Oscar Wilde said, "Hearts are made to be broken,"[1] which is why Oscar Wilde can kiss my shorn ass.

I once had a breakup. (Cut to me in my Ford Fusion singing "All by Myself" with Celine Dion. 🥺🚙🎤) When our relationship had run its course, **we took it off life support and called it quits**. A week later, we got out the defibrillator paddles, yelled, "CLEAR!" and tried to resuscitate it. Why? Because we didn't want it to be over. We loved each other and thought we could work it out, blah, blah, blah. For the next several months, we did our best to stitch things back together, but deep down, **we both knew our love story was over**.

Before we got together, I had five nonnegotiables for the man of my dreams. Although each was important to me, I realized within our first month together that he didn't quite meet two of them; I decided to let it slide. Did I mention I loved him? 🚩🙈🚩

That's the thing about love—it can turn us into hypocrites if we're not careful. **We'll compromise on those things we need to live our best lives**, essentially telling ourselves, **"You're not worthy of the love you desire."**

It takes courage to end a relationship that's no longer working, **especially** when we still love them. But if you're going to find the gay man you're meant to be with—the kind worth keeping—**you might need to let go of a love that is no longer working, or maybe never has**.

It could be time to break up.

If breaking up is what's next, get out your red Sharpie ✍ and circle this list.

- Therapist
- Friends who get it
- Bucket of fried chicken
- Celine Dion (Ford Fusion optional)
- Soft pajamas
- Netflix, Hulu, YouTube, Prime Video, Max
- Pizza
- Gym membership
- A copy of *How to Find and Keep a Gay Man*
- Cozy bed
- Blankets
- TikTok and IG Reels
- Ice cream
- All the patience you can muster, sweetcakes.

This is your breakup survival kit.

You can do this. And you're worth it. Why?

Because you deserve a meaningful love.

But first–the hard part: **the breakup**.

Hang in there, gayboy.

5 WAYS TO GET THE MOST OUT OF YOUR THERAPY SESSIONS

1. BE OPEN AND HONEST

Share Your True Feelings: Don't hold back your emotions or thoughts. The more honest you are, the more your therapist can help.

Discuss All Topics: Even if something seems trivial or embarrassing, bringing it up can be crucial to your progress. I have a "friend" who went to therapy for years and never told his therapist he was gay. (Talk amongst ya'selves.)

2. SET CLEAR GOALS

Identify What You Want to Achieve: Before each session, think about what you want to accomplish, whether it's resolving a specific issue or working on a broader goal.

Review Progress: Regularly check in on your goals and adjust them as needed with your therapist's guidance.

3. PREPARE FOR EACH SESSION

Reflect on Your Week: Think about any significant events, emotions, or thoughts that occurred since your last session.

Write Down Key Points: Jot down any important topics you want to discuss or questions you have for your therapist. This guarantees a more productive session.

4. ACTIVELY PARTICIPATE

Engage in the Conversation: Actively listen and respond during your session. Ask questions if something is unclear.

Complete Assignments: If your therapist gives you exercises or homework, make an effort to complete them, as they can enhance your progress. Don't waste your time.

5. APPLY WHAT YOU LEARN

Practice New Skills: Knowledge is power, but practicing new strategies is what brings change. Implement the techniques you learn in therapy in your daily life.

Reflect on Changes: Notice any changes in your behavior or thinking patterns and discuss these with your therapist or a good friend to better understand your growth.

We go to therapy to experience CHANGE. Remember, you will get out of it what you put into it. Make the most of your therapy sessions and enhance your overall well-being.

25

#BUSY

While out for coffee, I shared with my friend Meg the story of Catfish Connor and how awful gay dating can be. In the middle of my tear-jerker about this beautiful app boy who catfished me for two weeks, Meg rolled her eyes and blurted out...

"Oh my God, Matt, you are **SO BUSY**!"

I paused, while she sipped the foam from her latte. *Is she frustrated?* I wondered. *She seems frustrated.*

As I opened my mouth to continue telling my sad story, Meg set her cup down, leaned across the table, and said, "We're not doing this today, honey, because **you are BUSY**!"

"What in the fresh hell are you talking about? I'm not busy. I spend most nights with my succulents, eating frozen pizza, and watching *Will & Grace* reruns."

Then it hit me—Meg was imparting a bit of bitchy wisdom: *Snap out of it! Mind over matter. There are things to see, feel, do. Become the person you desire to be and MOVE ON!*

But I'm not much of a "mind over matter" gay. I'm more of a "let's do a deep dive into this fagotty pile of broken dreams and get it all over ourselves" gay.

After my coffee date with Meg, whenever I posted something on social media that sounded too emotional or needy, she'd comment: **#BUSY**. It was her not-so-subtle reminder that it was time to **MOVE ON**.

The truth: I had just gone through a breakup, and grieving was part of the process. But I was also twisting that grief into a broader narrative about how dating, the world, and even **LOVE ITSELF** were against me. But none of it was true. **The world, the universe, and love had always been on my side**—I just needed to align myself with them.

I want you to know that I understand—I know what a broken heart feels like. And maybe you're not okay right now. But my god, you gorgeous gay man—you *will* be okay. Know why?

Because honey, **YOU ARE BUSY**! 🦄

#1

MOVE THE FUCK ON.

#2

WRECKS ARE FOR REALITY SHOWS. NOT YOUR LOVE LIFE.

26
Wreck

Please tell me you're not still messing around with that wreck of a human being.

Yeah, yeah...cute as Joe Jonas. I don't care. **It's over and you know it's over.**

SO MOVE THE FUCK ON.

Awww...I love you.

Byeeee. ✌

27 Graduation & Letting Go

Yesterday, I received a photo in a text message. It was my ex-boyfriend in a cap and gown, snapping a selfie at his college graduation. He sent it with this message:

"Thank you for encouraging me to go back."

Years earlier, when we first met, he told me he wanted to go back to school. I told him he had what it took and offered guidance on how to make it happen. Nearly three years later, when we broke up, I was as heartbroken as I'd ever been **because I loved him deeply**. And now here he was, **expressing gratitude for something beautiful that came from our relationship**.

Deep down, I knew the main reason I came into his life: **to show him what real love was supposed to be**. What I didn't realize was that he came into mine **to give me a safe place to land in the wonderful world of the LGBTQIA+ community**. For a time, we needed each other. And then it was over.

Letting go of a seasonal relationship isn't just the *right thing* to do–it's the *best thing* to do. How else will we find the great love we've been hoping for, the love we're meant for, **the love we deserve**?

For me, the photo isn't just a snapshot of his graduation; it symbolizes mine too. We shared a beautiful moment together–brief but meaningful. We honored each other as best we could, and then **we let go**...or were pried apart. That part doesn't matter anymore, because we've both moved on to something better for each of us.

Letting love go **TOOK EVERY BIT OF STRENGTH I HAD.** I'll never forget how painful it was, but it was also necessary. It was the only way to my forever man, and I wouldn't change that for the world.

SO,
I LOVE YOU
BECAUSE
THE ENTIRE
UNIVERSE
CONSPIRED
TO HELP ME
FIND YOU.

—PAULO COELHO

PART V

Finding the Good Guys

My glorious fagaroos, "finding the good guys" isn't just about snagging any man; it's about attracting the kind of man who lights you up from within. We're going deep into the lessons learned in junior high gym, the qualities that make you irresistibly you, and the selfless acts that define true love. It's time to take off the mask, cast it aside, and be known for what matters most—how well you live and love. Ready to find your good guy? He's out there. But first, let's be sure you're prepared to meet him as your most authentic self.

I HATE THE WORD *HOMOPHOBIA*. IT'S NOT A PHOBIA. YOU'RE NOT SCARED. YOU'RE AN ASSHOLE.

—ATTRIBUTED TO MORGAN FREEMAN

28

Junior High

I can still feel it in my bones. Can you?

It's where you first learned **you weren't a man**–where you first believed **you'd never be a real man**. Probably in gym class. Or the locker room.

It isn't true. And it never was.

Can I tell you something? **You are not a caricature. You were never meant to be a stereotype.** You can stop acting the way they expect you to act anytime you want.

Be femme all day long. **If that's who you are—amazing.** If you're butch, perfect. If you would "pass for straight," good for you. If you'd have a better chance delivering twins than passing for straight, that's great too. Just don't change how you speak, act, or walk to fit in, stand out, or **HIDE** who you are.

REAL is what we're after—the REAL you. Not a version. No

Auto-Tune. No impostor syndrome. No Mask. **REAL.** Know thyself and honor thyself by **BEING thyself**. Period.

You want a man? **You want a lasting relationship built on love, respect, and honesty?** Then you need to be real.

So...

Get in a room with that junior high school boy and **TELL HIM THE TRUTH**—that he's not "less than." That he's not weak or wrong for who he is. That he doesn't need to exaggerate his personality or tone himself down to belong.

He doesn't need to hide.

He belongs in this world, **but ONLY as himself**.

I fucking LOVE Cher. Even dressed up as her for Halloween once. But I'm not Cher every damn day. All the other days, I'm me.

Be you. **Because YOU are amazing.**

29

Would You Be Nice?

At the beginning of a relationship, we show up as our best selves–exuberant, selfless, and great listeners. We're like, **THIS IS ME**! (Sorta.)

It's not that we're trying to fool anyone. In the honeymoon phase of a relationship, oxytocin and a desire to bond are running full throttle, which is why we tend to put our best foot forward.

But what happens when the newness wears off–when things stop feeling fresh and fun? This is often when the niceties begin to fade and we get right back to putting *ourselves* first.

At this very moment, my husband is making breakfast, stirring something egg-adjacent with a wooden spoon. Earlier, I made the bed and brought him his coffee. I love that he does nice things for me, and **I LOVE that I get to do them in return**.

This kind of commitment takes work, **but when selflessness**

becomes part of our daily routine, expressing love through actions becomes second nature—as it should.

But you don't understand. My life is crazy. I don't have time to put someone else first.

Yes, thank you for your honesty. **This next part, I say with love...**

You've literally watched 153 episodes of *Drag Race*. You have the time. **Because if you want to find and keep your gay man**, this is how it's done. #PeriodAndIMeantIt

We're on a mission, Mr. Crazy Life—**a mission to find and keep a gay man**. Wanna find a good one? Then ask yourself, **"What is it worth?"**

Would you be selfless? Would you be considerate?

Would you be nice?

Because if you won't, I promise you, **someone else will**.

30

Known for Love

An older gay gentleman once told me that in his younger years, he was "known for sex." Perhaps by an old bottle of Lubriderm. Or a ham sandwich he seduced when he was fourteen. 🙄 I listened as he spun his tale of satisfied sexual partners, followed by his fear of getting back in the game. His main concern? That he wouldn't be able to perform sexually like he did back when he was "known for sex." He was nearly a hundred.

Personally, I'm not known for sex—never have been. **I'm known for showing up for friends.** For knowing when to keep my mouth shut and when to offer advice. I'm known for making music. For being passionate. For loving people well. And for a good laugh or two.

How about you? What makes you interesting? **What sets you apart?** These aren't things you have to search for. They're things that were hardwired into you before you popped out of your momma's whatnot.

Are you smart? Daring? Fun? Compassionate? Hospitable? A thrill seeker? Artistic? Do you love animals? Do you know your way around a kitchen?

Last night, at 3:25 a.m., Christopher rolled over, kissed my forehead, and said, "Hi, sweetie."

This is why I married him—shit like this and so much more. Because even when he's half dead to the world, I'm still in that world, and he kisses me and calls me "sweetie." It's just one of the many things he brings to the table. **My sweet Christopher is known for love.**

What about you? **What are you known for?** What beautiful thing are you capable of bringing into a relationship?

LOVE ISN'T A PERFORMANCE.

IT'S A PRESENCE.

31

Jimmy Garoppolo 🏈😊

When the game happens to be on (which is almost never), I sometimes catch myself staring at Jimmy Garoppolo.

Just me? Am I the only one? **Why is he so easy on the eyes?**

Now listen–this essay won't help you find *or* keep a gay man, but I thought it'd be a great way to wrap up Book 1 of *How to Find and Keep a Gay Man*. Plus, I think I've earned one tiny little moment of self-indulgence for working so damn hard at helping you boys find the man of your dreams.

Now, where was I?

Ah yes...**JIMMY GAROPPOLO**. God. And wow. Not so great at throwing long, but easy AF on the eyes.

That's all. Jimmy Garoppolo. Cute as pie. **Though not as cute as Babycakes.** Not even close.

Okay then...

Now that you know how to **FIND** a gay man, it's time to learn how to **KEEP** him!

You ready?

Perfect!

ON TO BOOK 2!

HOW TO KEEP A GAY MAN

IT TAKES COURAGE TO GROW UP AND BECOME WHO YOU REALLY ARE.

—E. E. CUMMINGS

PART I

Get a (Real) Life

Let's get one thing straight–well, gay. Authenticity is the X factor in any great relationship. Pretending, performing, or filtering yourself might work on Instagram, but it won't *keep* a man in your bed...**or in your life**. Real connection doesn't come from curated perfection–it comes from showing up as your sometimes messy, always human self. Whether it's sopping up dog vomit, turning off the porn, or accepting **that your best days AREN'T behind you**, being real is how you find *and keep* love. So let's dive in, queens, because it's time to get real. For you. For him. For love.

32

Good Pairing

Before we dive into what it takes to **KEEP** a gay man, let's hit pause and make sure the foundation is solid. To be able to keep a gay man, you must first be paired with someone who brings out the best in you—who knows, understands, and loves you for you. Keeping a gay man isn't only about being real; **it's about good pairing**. So let's start there.

As I've already mentioned, I was straight married for twenty-three years. Beyond the challenge of being a gay guy trying to play it straight, there were other obstacles. My first marriage is what I'd call a bad pairing. **We were simply too different for the kind of ease that is the hallmark of a lasting relationship.**

If you're going to find and keep a gay man, **pairing is everything,** which is why it's important to ask yourself this question:

What kind of person am I?

If you thrive on hanging out with friends, love loud music, lavish vacations, and high-adrenaline activities, pairing with someone whose idea of a great weekend is ordering DoorDash and binge-watching *Gilmore Girls* **could be a breeding ground for resentment and an unfulfilling relationship**.

So what do you need in a partner? Also, what do you WANT? (Gentle reminder to stay out of the shallows.) I've shared my list of non-negotiables, which had nothing to do with his job, chest hair pattern, or whether he was an elder in the Church of Scientology. But it's *your* list, so write it down.

Take a few minutes now and make your list.

How many things should be on it?

Ten is too many. Two is not enough. Aim for four to seven.

Okay. What next?

Let your list marinate for a few days to a few weeks; then **SHARE** it with a good friend, your family, or your therapist and ask for their feedback. Receiving input from someone who knows you well is important, **because we all have blind spots**, and people close to us will often see things we can't. Once they've reviewed it, **revise your list until it feels right to you**.

One more thing about nonnegotiables.

As you lean into your list, you might think, *How do I know if my nonnegotiables are coming from a healthy, constructive place?*

Well, you little smarty-pants. 🤓 **That's an EXCELLENT question!**

Nonnegotiables are informed by our lived experience in relationships with others. If we've been paying attention, we've learned which traits work for us and which don't.

If a nonnegotiable comes from a place of self-love:

I know what I need. I know what's best for me.

...that's fantastic! But if it's rooted in resentment, pettiness, or hatred:

SO WHAT DO YOU NEED IN A PARTNER?

ALSO, WHAT DO YOU WANT?

I know what I DON'T need, and I also know WHO IS THE ACTUAL WORST!

...that's a different story.

If you find yourself writing your list in a fit of rage—your glitter pen tearing through the pages of your My Little Pony sticker journal—it's time to step away and get a Thorazine drip.

Healthy nonnegotiables are about you, not them. They aren't accusatory or angry, and they shouldn't be fear-based. **Make sure your list is about what's in front of you, not what's behind you.** Meaning, yes, learn from the past, but prioritize what you need TODAY.

Once your list is complete, **filter every dating prospect through it**. It could take a little time to know if someone is a match, so be patient...**but DO NOT compromise**. Because the things on your list **are essential to creating your best life**.

The goal is a healthy, happy experience that works for *both of you.* For this to happen, **good pairing is fundamental**.

One last word of bitchy wisdom.

MAKE SURE the things on your list are *actually yours.* This isn't about what your parents want for you, or what your friends want for you, or what society says is best for you. This is *your life.*

Your life. Your list.

Okay! Now that you've nailed down your nonnegotiables for finding your guy, it's time to focus on what comes next: **being real**. Because a relationship isn't just about finding the right guy—it's about the power of showing up as your true self. In a healthy relationship, authenticity isn't optional, friends; **it's FUNDAMENTAL for building a love that lasts**. So, let's dig in!

33

Stop Doing Porn

Hey there, Casanova. That naked dude on your screen—the one you think completes you—doesn't even know you exist. And guess what? He's been making bedroom eyes at every Dom, Dick, and Fairy with a Wi-Fi signal. So if you're already in a **REAL** relationship, why not take that sexual energy to the bedroom (or the kitchen or the backyard) **and give the porn a rest**.

Truth?

Research *overwhelmingly* shows that **regularly viewing pornography can trigger issues that lead to divorce or breakup, including lack of trust, emotional distance, sexual dissatisfaction, decreased sexual activity, insecurity, and overall relational instability**.[1]

And just to sweeten the deal, those boys you're watching aren't doing so well in their personal lives. **The porn industry is RIFE with sexual violence, coercion, addiction, STDs, and exploitation.** (I'm just here to help. At your service.)

It's not that big a deal.

Research says it is.

Watching porn is just what gay men do.

Unless they want to improve their chances of having a **more fulfilling relationship**. Turns out, love **DOES** cost a thing.

So the question is: **Is a steady stream of porn worth it**?

If your answer is *YUP!* you could be saying, *NOPE!* to the lifelong partner and meaningful love you've been trying to find. And if this is news to you, but you still don't plan to stop, **quit bitching about the lack of intimacy or effed-up emotional connection with your partner**.

If you've tried to stop watching porn but can't, there is help. **Call 1-800-NO-RUBBY** or visit **www.youaregoingtogoblind.com**.* Seriously though, I've been there. I've been sober from alcohol for eighteen years, so I get it. Quitting something that takes the edge off can be tough, and sometimes impossible to do alone. Alcohol was like that for me–it sat in my head all day, every day. It was controlling my life, so I did something about it.

There are meetings for porn addiction, same as for alcohol or drugs. If you need help, **Google that shit and GO**!

* Are these real? Of course not. But there's a special message waiting for you if you go to that link.

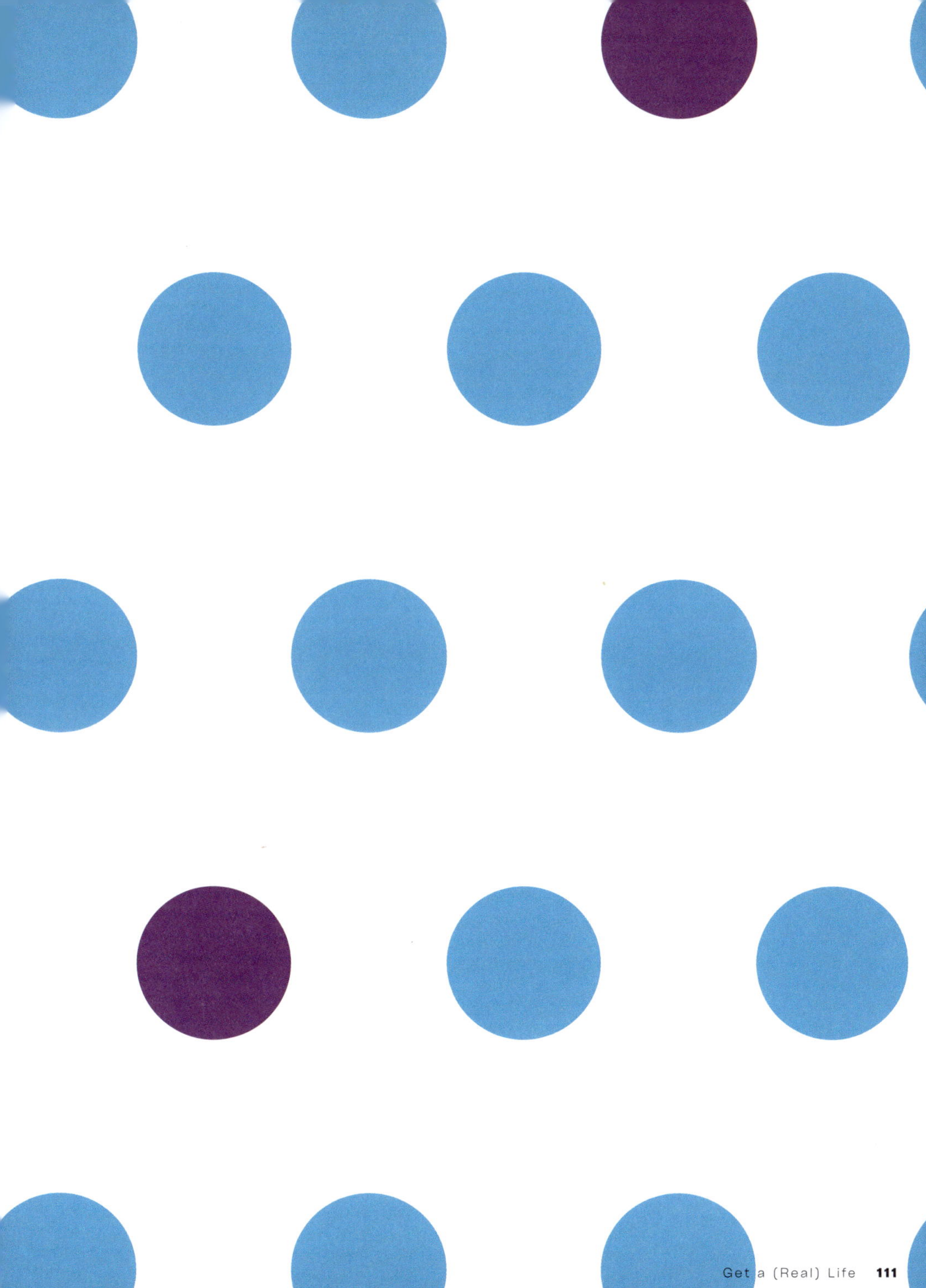

POP QUIZ: THE (NOT SO) FUNNY SIDE EFFECTS OF PORN ON RELATIONSHIPS

1. REGULARLY WATCHING PORN CAN LEAD TO:

a. Becoming an expert in fast-forwarding

b. Limited sexual activity and insecurity in your relationship

c. Carpal tunnel syndrome

2. IF THE PORN STAR ON THE SCREEN COMPLETES YOU...

a. Find his address and toss pebbles at his bedroom window

b. Expect to lose trust and emotional intimacy with your partner

c. Learn the art of one-sided, very awkward small talk

3. YOUR PARTNER COMPLAINS ABOUT A LACK OF EMOTIONAL CONNECTION. WHAT DO YOU DO?

a. Take it to a therapist or close friend or family member

b. Pretend to be asleep

c. Plan a "romantic" movie night and suggest *Saving Ryan's Privates*

4. WHAT'S AN EFFECTIVE WAY TO DAMAGE YOUR RELATIONSHIP?

a. Try a new hobby together

b. Spend quality time communicating

c. Watch porn together regularly

5. IF YOU CAN'T STOP WATCHING PORN AND IT'S AFFECTING YOUR RELATIONSHIP, YOU SHOULD:

a. Stop, drop, and roll

b. Call 1-800-NO-RUBBY or visit www.youaregoingtogoblind.com

c. Google information about Sex Addicts Anonymous (SAA), and get to a meeting

ANSWERS:

1. (b) Less sex, more insecurity
2. (b) Lose trust and emotional intimacy
3. (a) Take it to a therapist or close friend or family member
4. (c) Porn
5. (c) Sex Addicts Anonymous meeting

Maintaining a healthy relationship is more than just avoiding bad habits—it's about building good ones!

34

Accepting Reality

Jessica Simpson's debut song, "I Wanna Love You Forever," came out while I was still in the closet–and it made that closet feel just a little brighter.

Yesterday, I was hankering for some of those big belty Jessica Simpson high notes of yore and decided to take a trip down the anals of YouTube. (Because we're gay, honey. I don't make the rules.) Eventually, I unearthed a few old videos from when Jessica was the darling of *Divas Live*. (God, I'm so gay.) But that's not all I found. I also came across a more recent video of her *attempting* those same high notes, and well... Let's just say it didn't go well (which is a gentle way of saying it was tragic).

Dear YouTube,
You are the ruiner of dreams.
Sincerely,
Matt

We gay men love beautiful things—baubles, big voices, and all that glitters. We hope the beautiful things we love will stay beautiful forever. Jessica Simpson once did it for me—gorgeous, fun, sparkles, and whatnot. But her voice isn't what it used to be. It has changed. And that's okay—**because it was *supposed* to change**.

Know what else is changing? **WE are, darling.**

So what happens when we change? **Or when our partner does?** How do we accept ourselves and the ones we love when we're no longer as cute as we once were?

Gay men have worshipped at the altar of beauty since the Gayflower landed on Cape Cod. The problem with this is, by the time we hit our forties, many of us are holed up in our midcentury modern homes, awaiting the return of Jeebus. We think we've been replaced by all the young gay hotties. Well...

What if we have?

How do we LET THAT SHIT GO?

Those of us WISE ENOUGH to loosen our grip on the unrealistic beauty standards handed down by our gay predecessors—like the notion that our best days are behind us—have discovered a deeper, more meaningful purpose in life. But when our identity is still tied to clubbing, sex, and beauty, *we're living with an expiration date stamped on our ass.* And that's not cute.

We must learn to celebrate what *is*, not what *was*.

You're only young once!

It's true.

Accepting this reality might be difficult, but it's necessary if we ever hope to find lasting peace and happiness.

ATTENTION ALL DRAMA QUEENS... AUDITIONS HAVE BEEN CANCELED FOR TODAY.

—Anonymous

35

Drama Queen 👑

I know, I know... It's your personal brand. But your man is getting *real* tired of it. Maybe it's why he's no longer amused by your antics. Maybe it's why he's always hiding out in his home office or keeps coming home late from work.

Is he creating more and more space between you and him?

Remember when we used to go to theme parks, and some dude in ugly brown shorts would draw our caricature for fifteen dollars? So cute. It's not cute anymore.

Moral of the story: Don't be a caricature of a gay man.

This isn't about you being "too femme." If you want to dress exclusively from the *Delta Burke for Kohl's* collection, grind, honey–knuckle down. Love it. Love her. Here for it. 💁

It's **ALSO** not about you being the loudest queen in the room. So **YAWP** like a dead poet, Shakesqueer. 📣 We ain't mad at you.

THIS IS ABOUT you acting as if you're the ONLY QUEEN IN

THE ROOM—about your desperate need for **ALL EYES, ALL THE TIME**.

I've already told you my hubs is the nicest gay man on Earth—rolls his eyes just once a year. But let me tell you, there's this one queen who is really testing his limits.

We walk our city nearly every day, and like clockwork, we see her just outside a restaurant on our route. The minute she spots us, she yells, **"HEY BOYS!"** like she's handing out free mimosas at drag brunch. Then, *LOUDLY*, she starts rattling off every gay event happening that week: current drag shows, gay brunches, queer karaoke at the local Stick and Poke. Her performance is *clearly* not just for us. It's a show for everyone within a quarter-mile radius—a one-fag Pride parade.

She ends her not-brief-enough monologue with:

"I'll see you boys there!!!!"

This girl loves a scene...and *being* seen. It's a lot.

Listen, plenty of gays would love an evening out with Albert Goldman of *The Birdcage*. **But they don't want Albert Goldman every damn day.** So go ahead and turn it on at parties. Have yourself a gay ole time. Stick the battery in your gay jet pack and circle-snap to your heart's content. But knock that shit off when you get home, because he's not casting a leading lady.

He loves YOU. He wants YOU. Not the gay-hybrid drama queen you **INSIST** is just who you are.

Once upon a time, you were more than that.

BE MORE THAN THAT AGAIN.

36
Let's Get Vulnerable

Gays are notorious for being a controlling brood. Have you noticed? Maybe because we had to be–running from bullies, relying on wit over brawn, deciding to never feel small again.

Owning who we are used to be a struggle. It's possible (even likely) that since wandering the homophobic halls of high school, we've been overcompensating–gotten **REAL BIG**. Or maybe just real messy.

At thirty, my mantra was, *I don't care what anyone thinks of me.* Except that I did care–a lot. Back then, I struggled to see my own worth, to believe I deserved the life I dreamed of, or to find someone who'd love me just as I am. Loving myself and recognizing my value? I had no idea how to get there.

If there's one thing we've learned from the astonishing Brené Brown, it's that **vulnerability is a superpower**. Brené defines vulnerability as "uncertainty, risk, and **emotional exposure**,"[1] which is the *opposite* of control.

I think it's possible **we've lost sight of an important truth** that could help us become better versions of ourselves: **BEING HUMAN.** And vulnerability is at the CORE of humanness.

Being vulnerable isn't about lying on the floor in a heap with smeared mascara and a run in your hose. Being vulnerable is being honest, receiving and reciprocating selfless love, accepting when someone tells you no. **Vulnerability is about living life on life's terms.** It's about commitment—not just to another person, but to **WORKING ON YOURSELF**, which is the true source of our vulnerability.

Vulnerability is how you become real. And friends, **we do not find and keep a good gay man without it**.

So where do I begin?

I already know you have a therapist, so at your next appointment, instead of talking about what the girls at work said behind your back, or reliving your daddy issues for the eighty-third time, tell your therapist that **YOU'D LIKE TO BE REAL**. A **REAL** human being. And that you're ready to do the work, whatever it takes.

Healing requires more than knowledge—**it requires ACTION**. Transforming your life means *moving through it differently than you did before.* Simply put, you must stop doing the shit that has yielded poor results. And if for some reason you can't, find out why.

Start there.

37

The Good Stuff

Abbie the dog is old—and I mean **SO** old. At this exact moment, I can hear that sweet baby vomiting downstairs, which I'll be cleaning up during my next break.

Meanwhile, my husband's off to physical therapy. He's nursing a bad shoulder that's seen better days, which has made for some creative positioning in the bedroom.

ON TOP OF THAT...since Chris and I got married, I've moved to Cincinnati, switched careers, said goodbye to my support network, and have almost no friends.

It's been a BLAST.

But hey, this is life. Or real life. Or *my* life.

We're just up in our crib, hobbling for sex and sopping up dog vomit.

It ain't sexy—except yes, it is. **Because REAL life is REAL sexy.** Sexy as hell.

The funny thing is, it isn't what most of us dream of. But for those who want to find and keep a gay man, this is it. This is the shit. **THIS is the good stuff.** And I'm grateful for every second of it.

SHOUT-OUT to whoever is responsible **for this friendless, wondrous, vomitous goodness: THANK YOU!**

If this is what comes with my gay man...

I receive it all.

I accept it all.

I am *grateful* for it all.*

---

* RIP Abbie. You were such a gentle soul and a real sweetheart, except when people walked past your window. Get 'em! Good girl. 😔

The most inherently masculine thing I can do is throw caution to the wind and love you. ♥

—ANONYMOUS

PART II

Commit or Get (the Fuck) Out

II

Nothing says *forever* like a man who acknowledges you for exactly who you are. If he's tiptoeing around labels or calling you his "buddy" when introducing you to his family, no, honey. Commitment is about presence, honesty, and unapologetic authenticity. If he's making excuses, being ambiguous, or hiding behind "it's complicated," it's time to ask yourself: **Does this man truly see me? TRUE LOVE** means showing up for each other—the good, the bad, the ugly. It's choosing to believe the best in each other, even on the hard days. Putting him above all else, including your ego. Let's get clear on what you want and who you are. And if he can't commit to being real, be ready to sashay away. 💯

38

He's Not My Boyfriend; He's My Buddy

For years, I've hoped a friend of mine would find **REAL LOVE**. And guess what? Finally, he did. **He found a meaningful, genuine love.**

EXCITING, right?

But then he told me his new boyfriend refers to him as "my buddy" when talking to his family. As in, **"Can my buddy join us for dinner?"** or **"I'd like to bring my buddy on the family camping trip."** I swear, if I were his "buddy," I'd show up to that family camping trip in a leather catsuit and a pair of Betsey Johnson rhinestone whore-heeled booties.

I'd like to speak to a manager. I mean, for real... Girl, bye! 

If these boys were fifteen, I'd understand. But they're almost **forty**, which, IMHO, means they're headed for years of therapy—because **THIS IS ABOUT MORE THAN JUST BEING CLOSETED**.

If Hidey-McBridey won't acknowledge your relationship in front of his family, he's not fully acknowledging himself either. And we can't have that for you, cowboy. Especially if you're older. Why? **Because the clock is ticking.** ⏰

FIND A MAN who refers to you as his **BOYFRIEND**, not his **BUDDY**. And then make him your **HUSBAND**, not your **ROOMMATE**. 🙄

Say it with me...

"I'm not his friend; I'm his partner."

Louder, so the homophobes in the back can hear.

"I'm not his friend; I'm his MAN, his ROMEO, HIS HOMOSEXUAL LOVER!"

K thanks bye.

39

Flirting: When Does It Cross a Line?

When does flirting with someone who isn't your boyfriend, partner, or spouse cross a line?

This is important because flirting without boundaries could cause serious conflict in your relationship. Without getting the green light from your man, you could end up single and in your momma's basement watching *Queer as Folk* reruns all by your little lonesome.

For realsies tho. Honest question:

IS IT OKAY TO FLIRT WHEN YOU'RE IN A RELATIONSHIP?

Some might say, "Sure, it's human nature."

Others would say, "Only if he has a death wish."

Personally, I align with the "death wish" crowd. 🔪💧💀

I think we all unintentionally flirt. But what about when it's intentional? That's when we must **BE HONEST ABOUT OUR INTENTIONS**.

Don't tell your partner, "You're crazy. That wasn't flirting. He barely got my blouse off!" (We're not here for gaslighting.)

If you flirt (you whore), **establishing ground rules** is a top priority. **DO 👏 YOU 👏 HEAR 👏 ME?**

Why? Because a wandering eye without mutual understanding might be interpreted as, *He's lost interest. He wishes he was with someone else.*

COMMUNICATE. BE HONEST. And most of all... **RESPECT YOUR PARTNER'S DESIRE TO KEEP THE FLIRTING IN-HOUSE**.

If you find yourself having to convince him to accept your flirtatious behavior, it's probably not going to work. But if he's genuinely okay with it—feel free to proceed.

(Grab a pen. This next part is for free.)

If your wonderful, kind, godsend of a man doesn't want you flirting with others—if it's **THAT** important to him, it should be **THAT** important to you, boo boo.

Is flirting really worth the risk of losing him? If not, **protect that BIG LOVE**.

40

First Fight

Last night, the hubs and I had our first fight–not that it's any of your business. He currently has a side job that's taking up more of his time, and I've been missing him.

Here's how it went down.

Me: Honey, do you have a minute?

Him: (Pushes the computer away. Takes deep breath.) Sure. What's up?

Me: I need to talk to you about your schedule. Thank you for working so hard. I mean god, Chris, you are an amazing provider, and it means a lot to me. But all the extra hours–especially on the weekends–it isn't working for me. I'd like to find a solution that works for both of us.

(He pauses for thirty seconds, thinking about what I've said. I stay calm and give him the time he needs. Having presented myself calmly and clearly, I wait for his reply. Finally...)

Him: I think I need a little more time to think it over before I respond. Would that be okay?

Me: Of course, honey.

(He needed a minute, so I gave it to him.)

About an hour later, we were eating prepackaged ravioli from Trader Joe's. It was mostly quiet between us–a little uncomfortable, but manageable. After we finished, I took his plate, he kissed me on the cheek, and we shared the job of loading the dishwasher.

Just before bed, we had a longer discussion about work. There were no accusations **because we weren't looking for victims; we were looking for solutions**. Part of this is the blessing of maturity, though we know age doesn't guarantee it–some people just get old. But the hubs and I are committed to making this work. **FOREVER** is a shared value, so we approach issues and imbalances with **unconditional positive regard** and **openness**.

What about you? How do you approach disagreements in your relationship? Because how we handle conflict is a **VERY BIG DEAL**.

In the end, **I was proud of us**! 🤟

Without losing our shit–without pouting, codependency, manipulation, or guilt trips–this had been our very first fight.

41

"We're in an Open Relationship"

Permission to speak candidly. I don't know many who are built for open relationships. If you're in a forever relationship and want to continue fucking around, get after it—to thine own self be true. **But BE HONEST about it.** Don't pretend an open relationship is about being "woke," because open relationships are not a form of gay enlightenment.

Also, don't buy into the myth that being monogamous isn't possible—it absolutely is. Many a gay man will tell you about our supposed inability to "overcome our biology," as if we're just animals with no self-control. I'm not a fan of that mindset; it often feels like an excuse to justify bad behavior.

You want to have sex with people other than your partner—cool, cool. Tossing a handful of confetti your way. Just know that **this arrangement isn't congruent with stability, commitment, trust, longevity, intimacy, or keeping a gay man**. Studies have resulted in conflicting conclusions about open marriages and divorce, but several suggest that **open marriages have a 92 percent failure rate** compared to 50 percent for monogamous marriages.[1] That means that **opening your relationship could leave you with only a one in ten chance of its survival.**

Why? Because open relationships are a breeding ground for **insecurity, unfulfilled marriages, issues with time management, resentments, financial strain, and balancing the needs of multiple partners. They also OFTEN bring expectations and communication challenges with secondary partners, increased risk of STIs, and the potential for additional social stigma—which can lead to prejudice, job loss, or ostracization from friends and family.**[2] ← Google that shit right there. For the record, prejudice is never justified, but it's still out there.

Maybe George Michael was right; maybe sex **IS** best when it's one-on-one. Personally, I've never believed it should be a team sport...especially if you want to **KEEP** your gay man.

To the "I'm wired for it" peeps: Will it work for you? It's quite possible you have a one in ten chance, Kit-Kat. So think before you act. My advice? Ask yourself if wanting sex with someone other than your partner is truly about sex, or if there are deeper issues driving this desire. If so, it's important to understand what those issues are and if they can be fixed. Personally, I'd recommend doing a personal inventory *before* inviting Hot Young Pool Boy into your cabana. Good men have lost amazing life partners going down the open relationship path. To me, compromising a life-giving relationship for a little game of tickle butt is just...tragic.

To the "I'm NOT wired for it" peeps: Being monogamous does not make you a prude. If your boyfriend, partner, or husband is pressuring you into what feels like an indecent proposal, take your embroidery shears to his favorite caftan until he realizes you're not interested in third-party bits and pieces. If he won't let it go, ask yourself if it's time to walk away. Because if you are not wired for an open relationship, it simply means you are not wired for an open relationship. There's not a damn thing wrong with you.

As Queen Brené told us in *The Gifts of Imperfection*, "Fitting in is about assessing a situation and becoming who you need to be in order to be accepted. **Belonging**, on the other hand, doesn't require us to change who we are; it requires us to **be** who we are."[3]

If there's such a thing as a gay slam dunk, there 'twas, my little fagaroos. Know your limits and stick with them. Know who you are and keep being beautifully you!

42

Be Willing to Be Wrong

Jane Fonda once said, *"Consistency can be a trap, especially if it leads to being consistently wrong rather than to stopping, admitting your mistake, and changing course."*[1]

QUESTION: Do you make excuses when you're mean? Do you believe you have solid reasons for acting that way? Because let's be honest, few things are more annoying than a laundry list of justifications for bad behavior. Mean is bad. Mean is mean. In Jesus's name, amen.

A few years ago, a coaching client kept saying, "But I didn't **mean** to hurt his feelings." Okay, well, I didn't **mean** to drop a bowling ball on your foot, but I did, so I'm gonna say, "I'm sorry." If you've hurt someone—snapped at them, lied to them, been too self-absorbed, or hogged all the cookies—**RIGHT THE WRONG!** Make amends.

But vulnerability is hard for me.

I once touched a girl's boobies. The results are in: **We can do hard things**.

But I HATE being wrong!

Awww...neat story. Sounds like you'd rather be right than happy. Good luck with that.

The willingness to be wrong–**to OWN your shortcomings**–is a true indicator of emotional maturity, which is the stuff of healthy relationships. It isn't about apologizing. It's about acknowledging your mistakes or the hurt you've caused, then moving forward with the intention of creating new behavior patterns.

Here's a template for when you're in over your head.

"I regret that I *[insert shitty-ass thing you did]*. I can't change the past, but moving forward, I'm working to not behave this way again. I hope you can find it in your heart to forgive me."

THE END. Not another damn word. **SHUT IT, SHEILA!** 🤐

Why? Because this is about **THEM**. Don't make it about you by explaining yourself, adding background music, or throwing yourself a curtain call. 🎭

And finally...

If your guy doesn't forgive you immediately, be patient. Give it a minute. He might be waiting to see if your apology is followed with action. Remember, the focus shouldn't be on his response. Your primary goal isn't to get off the hook–it's to make things right.

We must keep the focus on what **WE** did, not what they did or how they reacted. We worry about *our side of the street.* Why? Because it's the only thing we have agency over, love.

When we're able to own our shit–when we're willing to be wrong–we aren't just making things right with them, we're **making things right with *ourselves*.**

43

Unconditional Positive Regard

The term *unconditional positive regard (UPR)* is credited to psychologist Carl Rogers. It refers to the practice of accepting and respecting others without judgment or evaluation. It is a core value for most therapists. UPR is a mindset–whether you think of it as giving the benefit of the doubt or assuming good intent, it's about viewing your partner through the most compassionate lens possible.

So if you walk past a steaming pile of dog vomit in the kitchen (which happened just this morning), and you're pretty sure **he** walked past it before you did, **unconditional positive regard** says...

He probably didn't have time to clean it up. Maybe he was running late. Maybe he had to throw his panties in the dryer before work. Or maybe he's planning to freeze it and use it as fertilizer next summer.

Unconditional positive regard will perform this level of psychological sorcery in service to love, which, when it comes to finding and keeping a gay man, is far better than thinking... *What an asshole!*

Turns out, my man had a big presentation at work and **WAS** running late.

Before leaving the house, he said, "Sorry about the dog vomit, honey. I've been stressed about my speech and needed to run through it one last time before heading in."

"No worries, sweetcheeks. You can get the next pile."

He kissed my face and was off to work.

This could've easily gone differently—no need to paint a picture. **But my man has stockpiled A LOT of love points.** He is selfless on the daily, so I knew he had a good reason for ignoring the mess.

Believing the best about my guy is a choice I make every day. For me, it's the right choice.

How about you?

44

Substance Abuse

Here's the awful truth: **20 to 30 percent of us are abusing substances** compared to 9 percent of the general population.[1]

We know why: **homophobia, discrimination, and mental health issues related to our sexual orientation**. Many of us also use poppers, meth, etc., to deal with tinkie issues in the bedroom, bathhouse, or back room at Trade. (***Tinkie:*** *Noun.* The male genital organ of higher vertebrates, carrying the duct for the transfer of sperm during copulation.[2] See also: ***Penis.*** 🍆)

If you're not interested in finding and keeping a gay man, fine—enjoy your sixteenth vodka Red Bull. **But if you want something deeper, know that living life buzzed (or worse) won't get you there.**

Personally, I've been sober from alcohol for eighteen years **because it was destroying my life**. I don't miss it. One thing I learned while in the throes of addiction is this: **ADDICTION DOESN'T DISCRIMINATE**.

It doesn't care if you're smart, rich, cute, talented, or great with people. **It will take everything good in your life and BURN IT TO THE GROUND.** (Where's the lie?)

Gratefully, with help and twelve little steps, I was able to let it go **because I refused to let addiction define my legacy**.

If you prefer living out of your mind, I don't love that journey for you, but still, I wish you well–go with Gaga. However, **if you suspect you might have a problem, GET HELP**! Good ole-fashioned **AA changed my life**. It made me presentable to the world, and most importantly, to myself. It provided tools and taught me to **take responsibility for my life:** the highs **and** lows.

The other day, I heard a gay guy at an AA meeting say, **"There are two things I hate: the way things are...and change."** But if we don't like the way things are, **change is necessary**.

For me, change meant getting sober. **What does it mean for you?**

BILLIONS OF PEOPLE HAVE HAD SEX.

I DON'T KNOW HOW MANY HAVE ACTUALLY MADE LOVE.

—SHEILA WRAY GREGOIRE

PART III

Sex & Sparks

Sex isn't just about wild nights or turning the bedroom into a Cirque du Soleil performance. It's about showing up as you are—the quirks *and* the weird morning breath. Whether you're laughing mid-orgasm, cuddling through the tough stuff, or spicing things up to keep that spark alive, true intimacy is what sustains a relationship. Forget the Hollywood version of romance; this is about something real. It's taking turns making breakfast, trying out a harness, or holding each other close when things get hard. Real connection isn't a shallow sex game—it's building a love that's beautifully imperfect and totally yours.

45
The Fucking Problem

When it comes to sex, men are often ego driven. It's like we're competing in a "dick pageant," and the judges have already begun deliberating. You're pretty sure you did well in evening wear, and you crushed the interview question, but in talent, your wrist wasn't the only thing that went limp.

So, what happens when you can't get it up anymore—either at all or the way you used to? What I'm really asking is...

DO YOU HAVE A FUCKING PROBLEM?

If you do, remember that it happens to the best of us. I get it. It's hard. 🤠

A queen once confided in me that she quit dating because, during her meth days, she was a sex god and didn't want to ruin her reputation. Yep—the same queen who was "known for sex." Her greatest fear? Not measuring up to her own sexual legacy. She too was afraid she'd pull a boner in talent—or *not* pull one, as it were.

LISTEN...

If you're with a guy of the "keep him" sort and sex is a struggle, *the Fucking Problem* can be frustrating as hell. **BUTT...**don't stop trying to find a solution. There are medications specifically designed for the burgeoning of the tinkie.

Your doctor has them.

GO GET THEM!

I've tried them. They don't work for me. Also, I'm a hundred.

Okay...just *SHHH.* Calm the fuck down. Now...where were we?

If you've tried everything–including therapy, since it's often a mental block rooted in past experiences–and you still can't seem to rise to the occasion, try exploring news way to create sexual intimacy. Lie together. Hold each other. Back rubs. Front rubs. Make out. But **STAY CLOSE**, because physical intimacy with your partner is important.

You want your relationship to make it? Keep connection. Keep intimacy.

KEEP SEX.

And as a gentle reminder for the porn-loving boys out there: if you're only having sexual issues in the bedroom and not in front of your computer, it's time to chat with a therapist or support group and get to the bottom of it. Before your *FUCKING* problem becomes a *FUCK-OFF* problem.

Sex IS
QUALITY OF
LOVE
NOT THE
ALIGN
OF YOUR

ABOUT THE

YOUR ENTIRE

LIFE

INTRICATE

MENT

BODIES.

—Kevin Leman

46

Eggs, Please!

So, you've found a new honey and you're all up in your feels. Fast-forward a couple years: the excitement fades; you're binge-watching all seventy-three episodes of *Game of Thrones* and romanticizing the good old days when you were ass-up in the bed of what's-his-name.

(You never remember. Sinner.)

Relationship ruts come for us all, which brings up the age-old question: **How do we keep love alive?** But first, a word from our sponsor.

Are you a fatalistic gay man? Have you subscribed to the cynical belief that relationships are "hard work" and then you die? Many a homosex didn't form strong relationships in childhood due to rejection from peers, parents, and Republicans. If that's you, a healthy relationship might be exactly what you need.

Therapy!

Therapy is for asshole-couples who want to understand each other better, form deeper, more meaningful relationships, and learn how to stop being assholes to their asshole partners.

THERAPY. (Insert herkie. **)**

Back to you, Matt.

Hey everyone. Me again. So, how **DO** we keep love alive?

Trust, support, friendship, communication–these are all essential for healthy romantic relationships. And each of these requires one thing above all else: **TIME.**

So...**CHANGE IT UP.**

Here's how: Tomorrow morning, get up and make breakfast–eggs, please! Brew some coffee and stay off your phone. Ask about his day and be genuinely interested. If he shares about an issue at work, ask how you can support him.

Other things you can do: Take a drive with the windows down. Get a new candle for the tub. Buy a harness. Plan something to look forward to, even if it's just a long walk. And when there's a misunderstanding, always always always...unconditional positive regard.

Lather. Rinse. Repeat.

47

The Laughing Orgasm

I like sex. There, I said it. I'd walk across hot coals for it. Have lunch with JD Vance for it. **Cut off Ariana Grande's ponytail for it.** (Then wear it.) What I'm saying is, sex agrees with me.

LOVE IT.

When I stepped into the gay community, I wasn't sure what to expect. The gay movies showcased **sexual freedom, fun, and kink,** but it always seemed to happen in dating-land, not in long-term relationships. Which begs the question:

What about us committed gays?

Many committed couples I know are boring AF when it comes to sex. I mean, there they are, lounging on the couch next to the love of their life, scrolling through their phones when they could be scrolling through each other's panties.

We gays can be **VERY FOCUSED** when we want to be. **We GET**

SHIT DONE. So why not use that determination **to revive our sex lives**? Because humdrum sex is for the birds. Remember the way **his hands used to feel on your shoulders**? Or that time you tried "The Pinball Wizard?" (Look it up and do it. And post pics. And tag me.)

Did you forget what it's like **to be COMPLETELY OVERWHELMED by him**?

Why did we stop having great sex?

I know a guy who laughs when he orgasms–laughs his ass off. 😉 I think this is a perfect example of what sex should be like, **ESPECIALLY** in a relationship built on fidelity and trust.

If you're virile, partnered-up, and aren't having fulfilling, fun, meaningful sex...**FIX IT**! **Sex is a powerful way to connect and express love**.

It also signifies the unique bond you share with your guy–**something exclusively yours**! Just think about that...because **THAT is special**.

THAT is worth celebrating (in bed). 🍾🥂🛏

48

Play the Tape Forward

I went to the gym this morning—that's where I saw him. He was bearded, muscular, young, and made way too much 👀 contact. I was married to a woman for twenty-three years and didn't cheat. I'm certainly not going to start now, especially when I have this exceptional husband at home—smart, beautiful, sensitive, and incredibly supportive. No thanks, Beardy. 🧔 I'm all good over here.

The thing is, **we are gay men, and gay men are visual**—and, admittedly, a bit indulgent. Unfortunately (and unfairly), many of us have been led to believe that we lack control over our impulses. And I get it—we're human for sure. But in my experience, **gay men are also shrewd**.

One thing that helps me when life presents a tempting, honeylicious situation at the gym, mall, office, gas station, Walmart, Kmart, or Stein Mart, is **playing the tape forward**. If you're going to do it right, go big or go home. Think through the full experience.

Playing the tape forward means imagining what happens **AFTER** you've compromised your morals and hooked up with Mr. Right Now. Don't just focus on the sex: **his biceps, the small of his back, or big of his butt**. Think about what comes next: telling your partner and breaking his heart; your kids finding out and watching their world collapse; Crazy Hot Guy blowing up your phone, then standing outside your apartment at 2 a.m. with a boom box over his head, channeling his inner Lloyd Dobler; **or the devastating loss of the love of your life**—because that's how this escapade ends.

Go ahead and imagine super-hot sex with Beardy McGym-Rat. Exciting, right? But **KEEP THE TAPE ROLLING** in your little fantasy: **Sex. Elation. Guilt. Shame. Secrets revealed. Heartbreak. Separation or divorce. DEEP regret.** And finally...**DEATH**. (It's a bit dramatic, but we're all gay here, so... 🎬 🍿)

Long story short, **cheating is a cruel exchange** with no takebacks—**trading something monumental for something momentary**. It's an exercise in futility, and it isn't worth it.

So, whenever you wonder if it *might* be, **play the tape forward**.

49

Change It Up

I have a friend who claims he never watches TV—says it's a complete waste of time. Yet somehow, he can quote every season of *Drag Race*, *All Stars*, *Game of Thrones, Looking, Orange Is the New Black, Long Island Medium*, and every damn city in the Real Housewives franchise.

Why? **Because he watches TV**, and he watches it **A LOT**. It's what's he and his boyfriend do. They come home from work. **They watch TV.** They go to bed.

And SHOCKER—they're BORED. 🥱 (And I'm bored of them being bored. 😑)

Did you know boredom in a relationship can be more damaging than fighting? Yep. **BOREDOM IS A KILLER.** Studies show that **relating to your partner in overly repetitive ways can make your relationship feel like a chore.**[1] **WE NEED EXCITEMENT**—new strategies to keep things fresh. Because **NEW EXPERIENCES**

release feel-good shit in the brain. And feel-good shit is the shit of happy relationships.

So change it up!

Not sure where to start?

Get a hobby **and do it together**. Take dance lessons or cooking classes. Go camping or hiking.

But I don't camp!

You do now, honey. You camp like a full-blown nomad lesbian in a Subaru...**with maximum towing capacity**.

My podcast cohost and good, best Judy, Matt Heincker, once said of his relationship, "Whatever we're doing, we're having a good time." Key word: *whatever*. It doesn't matter what they're up to—they put their backs into it. Heincker and his husband, Ty, actively CHOOSE to enjoy life together—and so they do.

A couple of months ago, Chris and I were bored on a Sunday afternoon.

"Wanna go to a few open houses?"

"Why?"

"Just cuz."

"Okay." And we did.

Did we need a house? No. Were we looking to relocate? Nope. Are we nosey as fuck? *Ding-ding!* We love going through people's panty drawers.

Listen, sometimes being bored means you're comfortable, which is great. But sometimes it means your relationship is getting stagnant and death is looming. **KNOW THE DIFFERENCE.** If the latter is true, take action. Get your asses to the dollar spot at Target and buy each other goofy gifts. Cook a meal together. Paint each other's toenails. **DO SOMETHING.**

And remember, the way to get anything done is to simply do it. **If your relationship matters, dig in and figure it out**. No one is going to figure it for you.

Wanna keep your man for the long haul?

Change it up. Find a way. Make it happen.

A BORE IS SOMEONE WHO DEPRIVES YOU OF SOLITUDE WITHOUT PROVIDING YOU WITH COMPANY.

—Oscar Wilde

50 Slow Sex

Last night, I was exhausted after a long day. I crawled into bed, fully intending to sleep. TV off, alarm set, lights out, a kiss good night, drift off to sleep–that was the plan.

Well, that was *my* plan. That's not how it went down.

It's been a minute since I felt like I might scream in bed, but within an hour, I was **COMPLETELY OVERWHELMED** by my husband in the best way possible.

Because he took it slow.

And this morning...**I can't stop thinking about it**.

The images. The soft touches. The penetrating looks.

In the late '80s, George Michael said: **"SEX IS FUN."** And I agree.

But last night was **MORE** than just fun. It was raw. It was spiritual.

It was transcendent.

Slow sex requires focus, commitment, patience, selflessness, love, and surrender—all of which are more accessible when **your relationship is rooted in trust**.

Maybe "fun" is all you're aiming for—we've all been there. **"Let's fuck," can be a hot and amazing thing.** Just don't let it be the **ONLY** thing. Because slow sex is where we **REALLY SEE** the other person.

It's where we connect who WE are with who THEY are. And this very special kind of intimacy**—where we are truly known—**is how we keep 'em, boys.

It's also how we keep ourselves.

SEXUAL INHIBITIONS Q&A: LOSING YOUR SEXUAL INHIBITIONS WITH YOUR PARTNER

What's the first step to losing your sexual inhibitions with your partner?

Communicate openly about your desires and boundaries. If a sexual issue is holding you back, your partner should know what that is. Be specific. Don't talk in generalities. And if the first talk doesn't go well, try again. Talking about our personal sexual hang-ups can make us feel insecure. But those who TALK about them are the ones who OVERCOME them. Don't overthink it—say what you need to say.

What's a good way to build trust with your partner in the bedroom?

First and foremost, respect each other's limits and use safe words if necessary. Get cute with it. Maybe your safe word is "Mariah Carey!" Second, remember that building trust can be uncomfortable, which is survivable. Make sure to be honest and clear. The more you talk about sex, the less awkward things will become, and the more you will begin to trust your man.

How can you boost your confidence during intimate moments?

So many things come to mind. Practice self-care and positive self-talk.

(Remember, we aren't measuring ourselves against Hollywood.) Keep foreplay light, fun, and KEEP TALKING to each other. If you're uncomfortable, nervous, or don't like something he's doing, SAY SO. If you love something he's doing, SAY SO. If you'd really like to try something, but are afraid, SAY SO. If you hate doing something he loves, SAY SO. When all the cards are all on the table, you'll both feel more confident.

How can you create a comfortable environment for exploring new things?

Set the mood with lighting, music, and a relaxing atmosphere. To avoid any awkwardness around hinting at sex, agree on a time for your sexual engagement. Simply say, "Could we connect tonight before we go to sleep?" Then spend thirty minutes preparing before bed: take a shower, shave things and rub lotion on them, brush your teeth, meditate. REACH FOR CONFIDENCE. If things don't go perfectly, don't be too hard on yourselves. The goal isn't perfection—it's intimacy, and that takes time.

What if I still feel sexually inhibited?

Consider attending an intimacy retreat or conference. Tell them you want to get to the root cause and create a therapeutic plan for losing your inhibitions in the bedroom. Nothing should be left unsaid—**say what you need to say**.

By applying these tips and OPENLY discussing them with your partner, you'll begin to let go of sexual inhibitions and move toward a more fulfilling relationship.

51 I Have a Question

When was the last time you lit a candle? When was the last time you took a bath together? When was the last time you had a weekend getaway or vacation for just the two of you? When was the last time you kissed for more than five seconds? When was the last time you sucked and fucked him? When was the last time you lay on the couch together (phones in the other room) and watched a movie? When was the last time you held hands in the car? When was the last time you wrote him a love letter?

When was the last time you reminisced about the day you met or fell in love? When was the last time you looked him square in the eyes and told him all the good things? When was the last time you sat with a friend and bragged about how amazing he is? When was the last time you made breakfast in bed for him? When was the last time you bought him a card that wasn't for his birthday? When was the last time you put out the trash so he wouldn't have to? When was the last time you hugged him and held on? When was the last time *he* hugged *you* and you *let him* hold on? When was the last time you really looked at him—his face, his calves, his elbows, the small of his back, his thighs, his lips?

When was the last time you *saw* him?

When was the last time you held him as he cried? When was the last time you promised you'd never leave? When was the last time you surprised him with new underwear? Or went out of your way to do something for him, even when it wasn't easy for you? When was the last time you gave him a massage? Rubbed his feet? His hands? When was the last time you saved the last bite for him?

When was the last time you told him how much you love him?

When?

When, friend?

When was the last time?   

Queer people don't grow up as ourselves; we grow up playing a version of ourselves that sacrifices authenticity to minimize humiliation and prejudice.

The massive task of our adult lives is to unpick which parts of ourselves are TRULY US and which parts we've created to protect us.

—ALEXANDER LEON

PART IV

Fix Your Shit

Sometimes the biggest barrier to finding and keeping love isn't the world around us–it's the baggage we haven't dealt with on the inside. In this section, we're getting real about doing our work: letting go of old hurts, healing wounds, breaking patterns, and understanding our worth without needing someone else to prove it. If you're here to find a love that lasts, you can't drag a bunch of unfinished business into it. Get ready to dig deep and confront the hot mess in your heart. Fixing your shit isn't easy, but it's the **only way** to make room for the kind of love you've been searching for. *This section of the book is my favorite–it's what I'm all about. And now, it's what you're all about, too, sweetheart.* ♡

52 More Than You Could Ever Ask For or Imagine

I'm sitting in a coffee shop in SoHo, NYC, listening to a song called "In the Meantime." When I arrived, it was my plan to write fun, quippy gay things for you to read—another cute little essay on how to find and keep a gay man. But since putting in my headphones, this song won't leave me alone with its lilting melody and haunting lyrics.

> **Hey baby, do you remember when I said**
> **I would give you more than you could ever ask or imagine?**
> **I wasn't playing, I wasn't playing with you, baby**
> **I'm the one in control, You're the one that I'm holding**
> **I'll take your burdens on my shoulders and carry us on.**
>
> **—Jess Ray**[1]

I wonder if you believe in God—many gods or just one. The universe, or yourself. Or your sweet little grandma who loved you so.

Whatever entity or person has shown you the most love—listen to *that* voice. That's the voice that will always tell you what to do, who you are, **how much you are loved**.

You're searching for a man. You want a *real* relationship. You want a love that will go on and on before burning out like a shooting star. You hope, when all is said and done, to go out of this world having loved someone...someone you've loved for a lifetime, because your love stood the test of time.

We've had a lot of fun moments here, and there's plenty ahead. But when it comes to true love, here's what I believe: *Someone or something wants to get a meaningful love to you—more than you could ever ask or imagine.* But you must receive it, which is the harder part.

But how do I open myself to it?

My darling, you already know. You've always known how to let love in.

Go on now, turn the page. We'll talk a bit more. Let's remember this very important truth together.

53 Worthy

Your inherent worth was imprinted on your gay heart the day you came into this beautifully chaotic world.

And Love? She was always here. **LOVE** was waiting. Always waiting—**IS** waiting—for you.

We must continue to stumble toward her—to scrape our hands and knees if necessary.

Not too long ago, my life revolved around caring for others more than myself. I was the textbook definition of *codependent*—always the 3 a.m. friend, the devoted husband, the ever-reliable father. I believed my worth was tied to how much I did for others, and that I only deserved good things based on my actions.

Shortly after Chris and I met, we got married. But I was still me—still codependent—which became a problem. Before Chris came into my life, **I USED LOVE to control outcomes and rescue people**. But

Chris didn't need rescuing. He was already a healthy, whole, independent man.

Which meant...

He didn't **need** me. He **WANTED** me.

At first, I was uneasy. I wasn't used to this kind of relational equity. But it turned out to be a beautiful opportunity to discover my worth—not through what I did for others, but simply by *being myself*. It nudged me toward the hard work of truly believing—deep in my bones—that I was enough.

Today, I'm still working to let this truth in. I know I won't have the love story I desire without believing I'm worthy of it. Period. Full stop.

I deserve a meaningful love...and so do you.

Now let's get even more honest. Turn the page.

54

I'll Show You Mine If You Show Me Yours

I grew up in abject dysfunction. Two boys and one girl—all of us abused in every way. Years later, my brother died in a motorcycle accident. He was twenty-three. Then my sister lost her battle with breast cancer. She was fifty-two. I don't know if either of them made peace with what happened to us as children before they passed, **and so a part of me has always felt responsible to find peace FOR them**.

Survivor's guilt is when someone feels emotional stress for surviving an incident in which others died. When my life began to improve, I wondered: *Why do I get this life of goodness, peace, and love when they deserved it too?* Instead of feeling grateful, **I struggled with feelings of unworthiness**.

Work will prove my worth. Rescuing people will add value. This is what I told myself.

Like some sort of day trader, **I bartered for my worthiness**. But it seemed like whatever I purchased with my love was used up by the end of the day.

This constant buying, selling, and trading of myself defined how I related to others for too long. No wonder I felt unworthy when my husband didn't need me to rescue or fix him. The idea that I couldn't "earn" his love seemed ridiculous—sometimes it still does. And ladies, this broken mindset **must be healed**.

My current job is to accept that I'm worthy of all that I've been given. If I don't, I run the risk of burning every good thing in my life to the ground. It's what I do. Can you relate?

Say it with me:

I will not fuck this up. I will not fuck this up. I absolutely WILL NOT fuck this up!

I can do something about it. **By seeking to understand it**, I already am.

What about you? Why is it so hard to believe that, beyond your talent, wit, charm, beauty, or success, **you deserve good things simply because you're alive**? What is keeping you from accepting this primal truth?

I showed you mine; now show me yours.

55
The Apology That Never Was

Friends, I know that sometimes we don't get the apologies we need from the people who've hurt us the most. If that's you, I want to offer this apology on their behalf. Imagine that these words belong to them, and let them flow through you.

I'm sorry I never learned how to love you the way you needed to be loved.

I am your mother, father, grandparent, sibling, minister, friend.

You've done something **SO BRAVE**–honored yourself by **BEING yourself**–and then found yourself alone. For that, **I am deeply sorry**.

I'm sorry I don't know what it means to truly *be* **sorry**. You'd be right to say I've failed to make the love I have for you about *you.*

Fear has twisted my love into something so small–that's the hard truth.

I'm afraid, and I am sorry.

But here's what you don't know:

My lack of empathy, compassion, and understanding has **NOTHING TO DO WITH WHO YOU ARE**, and **EVERYTHING TO DO WITH WHO I AM**.

My higher self knows this.

Even though this broken version of me—the one standing before you—hasn't figured it out.

And what's worse, I don't know if I will.

I don't know if I *ever* will.

So here's what my **HIGHER SELF** wishes for you:

Chosen family. You're going to need it, love...**so choose wisely**.

Choose people who see you, who honor the beauty of who you truly are—not who you once pretended to be.

Choose people who bring strength, joy, love, acceptance, accountability, hope, and faith into your life.

Choose those who will be stronger for you than I've been.

Also, I wish for you a great and meaningful love.

Someone who completes the beautiful parts of you I couldn't understand.

And when that person loves you the way you always deserved to be loved, please...

Remember me.

Know that if I were capable—**if I knew how**—I'd love you just the same. In a strange way—the way of mystery or fairy tales, the way of the universe, or god, or fate—*their* love is *my* love.

The love I just couldn't seem to find.

Is it bullshit that I couldn't find it?

That fear, or religious indoctrination, or shame held me back?

Yes. It is. One hundred percent.

But please—**for your own sake**—let the anger go.

Beyond the shame I've burdened you with, I want you to know the beauty of true freedom in your love.

I want your love—and your life—**to soar**. 

If it feels healthy to hold on to the hope that I'll get better someday—

Please, don't stop hoping.

But if that hope ever holds you back or slows your healing, know that it's okay to let me go.

I regret that I couldn't add strength to your wings, sweetheart.

Maybe one day I will.

But until then, know this:

At every family gathering without you—

Every birthday party or holiday spent in your absence—

These words will be etched into the unseen part of my heart:

I am sorry.

56
Get Alone in a Room with GOD

Whatever you conceive God to be–the universe, nature, or a gaggle of gays who really see you. For some, GOD stands for **G**ood **O**rderly **D**irection. Whatever it means to you, getting alone with God means *quieting your heart and listening for the truth that could set you free.*

We all want to love and be loved. It's one of our most primal human desires. I'd even call it a need. For some of us, the word "need" might feel uncomfortable because, as young gay boys, our needs often went unnoticed or unmet. It was easier to stop needing. Easier to figure things out on our own–to build walls instead of bridges, **to armor up and go it alone**.

But eventually, the self-protection stopped working, and we found ourselves isolated from meaningful connections. The bitchiness, one-night stands, exaggerated personalities, financial struggles, control issues, manipulative behavior, and substance abuse that many of us deal with are **DIRECT RESULTS** of the dysfunctional behaviors **we used**

to protect ourselves—to feel safe. Well guess what? It's not anyone's fault. We were doing our best. But now, it's time for a change.

How?

First, get alone in a room with God (whatever you conceive that to be) and **write out a list of all the unhealthy or dysfunctional things you've done**, or are still doing. Focus on the things **that are keeping you stuck**. If you're not sure where to begin, refer to the list in the previous paragraph for inspiration.

Second, share your list with a therapist or trusted friend, *admitting the exact nature of your wrongs.* Read your list out loud–it's important to *say* the words. This step is crucial.

Last...

Moving forward, **ASK FOR HELP**.

When faced with difficulties in relationships, seek accountability from your therapist or friends **and keep the focus on YOURSELF**, not on others. Remember, others were never your problem, buttercup–**YOU are your problem**.

Because if you're not the problem, there is no solution.

You deserve to be loved–that's the truth. But here's what is also true:

You're the only one standing in your way.

57 Hot Mess Clingy & the Push-Away Partner

I don't require much alone time. Honestly, **I could be with my man twenty-four seven**. It's not something I feel bad about, even if *Cosmopolitan* says I should feel bad about it. To all those online relationship clickbait magazines: **I shall not be shamed!** K, thanks, bye. 😘

We're all wired differently, which means **we require different amounts of time together or alone**. While on the lookout for a man, I searched for someone social, because that's who I am. I enjoy a good hang with my partner—not everyone does.

Can I be alone and at peace by myself? Of course. When I can't, I know there's a problem. If Chris leaves for an outing, meeting, or hobby and I'm not okay, it's means there's something in me that needs attention. **Because MISSING him is different from not knowing what to do with myself while he's gone.**

In the past, I had no problem with my partner leaving for the weekend or an afternoon. But after someone hurt me deeply, **I became much clingier in relationships as a direct result**. Well, guess what? That hurt got its ass taken to my goddamn therapist.

Now let's look at the flip side.

Perhaps you're the kind of guy who doesn't enjoy being with his man every minute of every day. Good to know, and not a damn thing wrong with it.

BUT...

Needing alone time is different from isolating. Taking time for yourself is healthy, whereas isolating or pushing your partner away often stems from avoidance.

Avoiding what?

Avoiding being vulnerable with another person.

Avoidance or isolation happens when people fear judgment from others, are uncomfortable addressing issues in their relationships, believe they're unworthy of connection, or use it as a means of coping with their feelings.

Don't overthink this. Deep down, **whatever the sitch**, you know if there's a problem because you can **FEEL** it.

So what do I do? (Awww, I just love when you ask for help. )

TWO THINGS:

Lose the expectation that your partner should just deal with it and unconditionally accept certain behaviors like isolation or clinginess as unchangeable traits.

GET HELP! Stop talking to your parakeet about it and seek out a *real solution.*

You don't need to fix the problem on your own. Because Google. Because therapy, darling. Now, get your ass to a therapist, and learn what it means to be **securely attached**.[1]

Pushing them away isn't cute. Neither is crawling into their suitcase when they're leaving for a business trip. (Might've tried this. Don't wanna talk about it.)

Hotmessclingy. 😉 Push-awaypartner. ✋ Therapist. 🧑‍⚕️ You. 🏃

Go get the help you need!

58

Codependence

If codependence were an Olympic sport, I'd be standing center stage, rocking the biggest gold medal you've ever seen. Then I'd share it with the silver and bronze medalists so they wouldn't feel bad.

If this sounds like you, babes, it's time to get it together, **because it isn't cute anymore**.

Can we get real? I'm not sure I'll ever completely eradicate codependence from my life. I've set fire to it more times than you can shake a stick at, yet it always manages to survive in some small sneaky way.

Some background on me: I'm a middle child. If you didn't already know, middle children often feel overlooked, which can lead to people-pleasing in an effort to gain approval. Left unchecked, this habit can spiral into a lack of boundaries, laying the foundation for codependent relationships. In past relationships, **codependence was a VERY BIG issue for me**. I've worked hard to manage it by developing a healthy internal monologue, seeking out accountability, and—most importantly—understanding what codependency actually is.

Okay then, what is it?

Glad you asked!

Codependency is a psychological pattern where an individual in a relationship becomes overly focused on the needs and behaviors of another person, **often at the expense of their own needs**. Typically codependence is characterized by low self-esteem, excessive caretaking, difficulty setting boundaries, and a strong desire to control or "fix" the other person. While not a formally diagnosed mental disorder, it is considered **a dysfunctional relationship dynamic that can significantly impact a person's well-being**.[1]

Here's what this means for me: **I can't heal or change anybody**. In fact, trying to is a complete waste of time. I can, however, change myself.

How?

BY REALIZING I'M JUST AS IMPORTANT AS EVERYONE ELSE.

When I was stuck in codependence, **it inevitably led to anxiety, low self-esteem, and a *Downton Abbey* marathon**. Understanding that **my worth wasn't tied to fixing someone else's life** became the biggest catalyst for change.

Now, listen up! 👂 📣

Codependent behavior is often an attempt **to validate our own existence**. If you're obsessing over someone else's problems instead of your own, it likely means you don't believe you are enough. But here's the truth: **you *are* enough**. Embracing this truth isn't always easy, but it's the best path I know out of codependency and into freedom.

Ringing any bells for you? PERFECT! Now, get to work.

There are resources available. The harshest motherfucking book

I've ever read on the subject is *Codependent No More*, by Melody Beattie.[2] (If you order it, know that Melody will be coming for your codependent ass.) Also, there are support groups like Co-Dependents Anonymous: CoDA.org. Check them out!

Remember, getting a handle on codependence is a process. Gay wasn't built in a day. There will be setbacks, which you'll share with your therapist because **YOU ARE GAY, SO GET A DAMN THERAPIST!**

Why is all of this important? Because if you remain stuck in codependence, keeping a **healthy** relationship will be unlikely.

Leaving you with a little bitchy wisdom...and please know this comes from a place of **DEEP understanding and personal experience**:

You can't fix anyone, love.

You never could.

You aren't the answer for them.

And you **never** will be.

59

Needy-Ass Bitch

Hubs has several dinner meetings this week. He's Business Boy, after all, which makes me an Executive Spouse. (Flips hair.) However, this Executive Spouse ate Chipotle while Babycakes and his sophisticated business colleagues enjoyed the Admiral's Feast from Red Lobster... probably.

What I'm trying to say is: I didn't get to go. **I would have loved to but didn't get to**. Not only that, but I had to deal with my feelings about this **ON MY OWN**.

I'm happy to report **no passive-aggressive nonsense**. I didn't mope around the house or pretend to take a handful of pills. Instead, I wished him well, and my ass folded laundry like a '50s housewife clinging to control one folded towel at a time.

I admit, sometimes I can be a needy-ass bitch. It's not cute, but it's real. I'm also very aware **THIS IS MY PROBLEM TO SOLVE**, not his. I mean, let's be honest: this is about more than not wanting to be home alone with my chips and guac. There's fear involved. Probably a little FOMO too.

Fear of what, Matt?

None of your beeswax—that's what. Certainly not anything about younger gay men who will be in attendance, if that's what you're getting at. Regardless, **WHATEVER** the problem, **that shit is MINE**. I cannot expect Chris to adjust to my emotions. When moments like this crop up, it's important for me to focus on myself. Because again, if I'm not the problem (say it with me), **THERE IS NO SOLUTION**!

When my honey returned from dinner, we crawled into bed, and he shared all about his evening. I especially enjoyed the story about the young gay boy with bad teeth and ring around the collar. My man had a good time—he always does. It's one of the many things I love about him.

When he finished his story, we turned on the TV, snuggled up, watched *Heartstopper*, and once again, all was well with the world. **I had survived the evening without him**.

He has another business dinner scheduled for tomorrow. He'll be taking the crew to eat at the AIRPORT HOWARD JOHNSON'S... probably. Once again, not invited.

Wish me luck as the newest server at the airport HoJo. 

60

Bored Man Seeks Personal Growth

Here's the thing about every relationship ever: **we get bored**. There's nothing wrong with a little boredom—love doesn't always need its own personal DJ.

I have a friend who's in a pretty chaotic relationship with...let's call him "Nancy." Nancy is intense. If he's not angry, he's sad. If he's not sad, he's ecstatic (IYKYK). Anyway, I'm pretty sure my friend would trade his vintage Jem doll for a boring relationship.

Boredom typically creeps into relationships after the honeymoon phase, which isn't a problem **unless we make OUR boredom OUR PARTNER'S fault**. Expecting our partner to always keep us interested, make us laugh, or maintain the same level of passion as when we first met is a recipe for trouble.

There is such a thing as GOOD boredom, which is about being settled, comfortable, and at peace. **Good boredom can also aid in**

the development of independence—fostering creativity and self-esteem.[1]

Of course, every relationship needs a shake-up now and then–a weekend getaway, reconnection, or new shared goal. **But we cannot expect *them* to make *us* happy.** If he's a nightmare to live with, I get it. But if he's a good guy and you're just bored, **that's a YOU problem, peanut face...and you could be flirting with codependence**, which we just talked about a few pages ago.

That said...

If you're bored, better yourself.

Personal growth is a lifelong journey of actively improving your skills, knowledge, goals, and personal perspective. There's not a thing in there about your guy not meeting your needs, or how he never blah-blah-blahs.

So...

Find a new challenge. Set new goals. Go back to school. Or just start small–switch your bedroom around or get a roll of bondage tape. Whatever it takes, find a way to challenge yourself. After all, you're the one who's bored, which means **the responsibility for being NOT bored belongs to YOU, not him**.

Now, sashay to the registrar's office, Nancy. Before you ruin a perfectly good relationship.

Byeee. 👋

LOVE HIM AND LET HIM LOVE YOU. DO YOU THINK ANYTHING ELSE UNDER HEAVEN REALLY MATTERS?

XOXO

—JAMES BALDWIN

PART V

Make It Last

Finding love is one thing; keeping it is another. This isn't about planning the perfect date night or being a rock star in bed (though both help). It's about showing up, day after day, with honesty, **GRATITUDE**, and the humility to say, "I'm sorry," when you screw up. If you want love that lasts, you've got to go deeper. Learn how to communicate, how to laugh, and even how to fight **in a way that makes you both stronger**. Relationships are messy, glorious things, and making them work takes effort, humor, and loads of forgiveness. So, hold on to your man, and be willing to do what it takes to keep the fire alive.

61
How Could You?

Can we talk about sex one more time? I know, right? Isn't it the best? When it's good, it's **SOOOO** good. 🔥

Well...

This isn't about that, Mr. Pushy-Tush. **This is about the awful thing you said to your partner yesterday.** 👆

Seriously, **how could you**?

Text him and say you're sorry.

I'm not kidding.

Text him **RIGHT now**. Not when he gets home. Not tomorrow. **NOW!!!**

But what do I say?

Try something like this...

Hey sweetie,

What I said last night... I hate that I said that to you. I opened my mouth and out it came. Whether or not it hurt you, it didn't come from a place of love. I was [angry, hurt, frustrated with, stressed about...]. Regardless, I was wrong for saying it, and I'm very sorry. Oh, and when you get home from work, my body also needs to apologize. It was very naughty and wants to make it up to you. 🤍🔥 Hope your day is going well. Looking forward to seeing you later. You are THE BEST. How'd I get so lucky?! MUAH! 💋

That's it. Eat a little crow, say nice things, and MEAN it.

62
Speak

If you're like me, saying what you need isn't easy. But in healthy, lasting relationships, **communicating your needs is fundamental**.

Growing up, it was easier not to need anything. Even twenty years later, asking for what I needed still felt unnatural. Sometimes, before speaking up, **I'd practice stating my needs IN FRONT OF THE BATHROOM MIRROR**—which was exhausting. Naturally, I'd follow it up with a little aromatherapy and light refreshments.

When we don't communicate our needs in a relationship, everything ends up on their terms—even when that's not what they want. This lack of communication often leads to **unmet needs, resentment, and the feeling of being invisible around our guy**.

Most people fall into one of two camps:

Those who ask for every damn thing they need.

Those who set themselves on fire to keep others warm.

Let's focus on the second group: **the ones who struggle to ask for what they need.**

Say these words out loud and fill in the blanks:

1. I would like to watch _______ tonight.
2. Could you help me with _______ when you get home?
3. Would you mind if we went to _______ for our anniversary?
4. I would really like for you to _______ before the end of the weekend.

The THREE MAIN REASONS we don't ask for help:

1. Pride. The male ego at its finest.
2. Fear. We're afraid of being a bother.
3. Gaslighting. We've been manipulated into believing our needs don't matter.

Which option best represents you?

Understanding **WHY** you struggle to ask for what you need will help clarify the best way forward. Whether it's pride, fear, or something else, get into therapy, find a support group, or Google the phrase, *how do I learn to speak up.*

Get familiar with the feeling in your body that tells you, *You have something important to say.* Learn to **SPEAK UP**! Expressing your needs in **healthy ways** is essential. The more you practice, the easier it becomes.

Resentment, fear, or feeling invisible can tank a gay relationship faster than a Grindr hookup. So, like I used to say to Mimi—my sweet little cocker spaniel who is now with Jesus:

Speak, bitch, speak! 

MY
SILENCES
HAVE NOT
PROTECTED ME.
YOUR
SILENCE
WILL NOT
PROTECT YOU.

—AUDRE LORDE

63

Fuck Me Sane

Yesterday, I helped my daughter settle into her new apartment—her mother and I worked together to give her a fresh start. It was the first time the two of us had spent any time together since our divorce over five years prior.

We worked hard for our girl, including the joint effort of getting an enormous 1960s couch up a narrow winding staircase, which we now call "The Miraculous Couch Experiment."

Situations like this can be stressful, especially with unresolved emotions. The couch making it up the stairs felt like a metaphor for our family almost making it.

Except we didn't. Except I was gay. Except there was a lot of pain.

On the drive back to Cincy, my head spun with thoughts like:

Life is hard. Relationships can be too. We're all human. We're all doing our best.

When I arrived home at 1:34 a.m., I crawled into bed with a fair amount of head trash from the day. Somewhere between half awake and half asleep, I felt my husband's feet touch mine, reminding me that I was home, in a safe place, **next to my person**.

When I woke up this morning, I was still feeling a bit conflicted. I went to the kitchen to get our coffee started. Soon after, Chris came downstairs, dragged me into the pantry, and worked me over pretty good. Then we migrated to the bedroom, where he fucked me back to sanity.

Lying here in the aftereffects, **nothing could kill this love buzz**. He made everything right. **He fucked me sane.** It's exactly what I needed.

In this marriage, neither of us is going anywhere, because we both show up for each other. Every damn time.

This is how you keep him, boys. This is how you keep your gay man.

64

Like a Prayer

I pray in bed—sometimes out loud. I don't know if there's anything out there. Most of the time I think there is; then at other times, I'm not so sure. Regardless, **I pray because it helps me. I don't believe it changes God, but I do think it aligns my spirit with what matters most to me.**

About six months ago, my Christopher, **who is sure he doesn't believe in God**, said a prayer out loud as we were going to sleep. **He prayed for me and for us.** Mostly, he just kept thanking whatever he doesn't believe in—for me.

I was moved by his prayer and felt so close to him.

More than anything, **I was just grateful**.

Prayer can do that—make you grateful. **And gratitude is a VERY attractive attribute.**

No one enjoys being around someone who is constantly grumbling about how horrible their life is, especially if that life was created from clubbing, cheating, and self-absorption.

Goddamn, Matt. Harsh much? Shit.

We all started asking God for things when we were kids. And now, as grown-ass gay men, **we should probably start thanking God for some things too**. Psychologists encourage gratitude because **it is consistently linked with positive emotions, better health, and** (wait for it) **STRONG RELATIONSHIPS**.*[1]

It doesn't need to be complicated. Start with the words, **"Thank you for…"** and stay there for a bit. You can add in, **"Help me with…"** eventually. But mostly, **stick with gratitude**.

Try it for a month.

Or forever.

See what happens.

---

* Harvard Medical School said this. You better pray, bitch! 

I THINK
GAY IS A
AND IT'S
I AM
FOR EVERY

BEING BLESSING, SOMETHING THANKFUL SINGLE DAY.

—ANDERSON COOPER

65

Who's the Cutest in the Room?

I had dinner with a gay couple last year. **They kept talking about the cute young waiter serving our table.** His eyes, his ass, his jawline—there was something new to discuss each time he returned.

You might think this kind of thing is harmless.

IT ISN'T.

A man worth keeping shouldn't have to wonder who has your attention—who's the hottest, most desirable, or most interesting.

So if your partner looks at a young waiter and says, "Remember when we were that young and beautiful?" A great response is...

"He's not cuter than you. You're the only beautiful thing I see here."

Is it true? **Make it true.** Does he believe you? **Who cares?**

This is a way for you to communicate something very important.

You're letting him know..."**YOU** are my man. **ONLY YOU.** You do it for me **100 percent**. **There will NEVER be anyone else.**"

These little affirmations **BUILD CONNECTEDNESS and LOVE ENERGY** between you.

If you saw the above exchange between a sweet old couple, you'd think it was totes adorbs, right? **BECAUSE IT IS.**

It's another way to make a deposit into your partner's love bank, so when you need to make a withdrawal, you won't get an "insufficient funds" message.

If you're reading straight through my little gay guidebook, you already know how I feel about Jimmy Garoppolo. You might've also noticed I made sure to mention he runs a distant second to Babycakes. No contest, really. It's an unfair battle. **Babycakes all day long.**

Now, tell me...

Who's the cutest in the room?

Your man is.

EVERY DAMN TIME.

NOW I LAY
SLEEP. I PRAY
AND NOT A
IF MY MAN IS
AND SWITCH,
TO GOD I
CUT A BITCH.

ME DOWN TO
FOR A MAN
CREEP. AND
A BAIT
I SWEAR
WILL
AMEN.

Hey, FAG, it's me.
I quoted myself.

66

Jealousy & Trust—Part 1

This morning, I was at the gym with my gay husband. Have I mentioned he's gay? Super happy about it. Anyway, while minding my business—doing push-ups like a good little queerling—I noticed a hot guy talking to Chris across the gym. **Instantly, I felt a twinge of fear**, which quickly spiraled into a crazy story in my head about their desire to be secret lovers. 🤐

After gathering myself, **I realized the fear I was feeling wasn't new**. My friend Laura likes to say, **"If it's hysterical, IT'S HISTORICAL."** 😯

"Hi. I'll take 'Rude Things' for five hundred, Alex."

Truth: Jealousy was never a part of my genetic code, right up until it was.

I was once in a relationship with someone who started hanging out with another guy—**A LOT**! I did all the usual things—talked to him about it, expressed my concern, burned an effigy into his lawn—but it continued. The psychological fuckery of this situation is what planted the seed. The jealousy I felt at the gym (hysterical) was just a flare-up of something old (historical).

The root of my jealousy?

FEAR OF ABANDONMENT.

Eventually, when our relationship ended, **I thought my issues with jealousy were over**.

THEY WEREN'T.

And since I wasn't healed up from it, **I carried that problem right into my marriage—which needed to be addressed**.

HERE'S WHAT HAPPENED:

While Chris was speaking to the hot guy (who was becoming less attractive by the moment), I continued my workout. **I didn't go over, make my presence known, or pee on his leg**. (Is anyone impressed besides me?) As they continued talking, I ducked into the empty cycling suite and prayed a very jealous, very desperate prayer.

At first, I told the universe how much I trusted Chris—but that didn't feel right. So instead, I began praying about **trusting myself**, which, to be honest, felt a little strange.

"Matt Bays," I whispered under my breath, **"I trust you. YOU are trustworthy."** Instantly, I felt a wave of relief wash over me, though I wasn't sure why.

When I returned home, I reached out to a friend, **because when I get stuck, I ask for help**.

For the very dramatic conclusion to the story of the E.T.-looking motherfucker at the gym who might've been hitting on my husband, but wasn't, but could have been, but didn't...**TURN THE PAGE**.

67

Jealousy & Trust—Part 2

What My Friend Said

As soon as I arrived home from the gym, I texted my friend Meghan.

> ME: Question. Today, I had to remind myself that Chris is trustworthy. Ever since the emotional complexities near the end of a previous relationship, trust has been an issue for me. So I took a moment and prayed out loud. "Chris is trustworthy. I trust Chris." At first, the prayer felt right, but then just as quickly, something felt off in the messaging. So I changed my prayer to "Matt Bays, I trust you. YOU are trustworthy." This new prayer felt much more powerful to me. So here's my question: Why was this the better prayer?

HER: Oh sweet holy mother. I'm gonna call you in five!

When she called, I told her all about Christopher's hideous wannabe lover at the gym.

Meghan is a *trauma* therapist, and while this was just a case of trauma *drama*, we agreed it qualified. I grabbed my computer, opened a Word doc, and wrote down everything she said.

Here is that exchange, word for word:

Here's why the second prayer was better, Bays. The most powerful inner-child work is going back for that wounded child with the skills of the adult you are NOW. You are connecting the child you WERE with the capable adult you are TODAY—who actually CAN be trusted, and CAN speak up for the wounded child. The "I can trust myself" prayer—that is NIRVANA, my friend. It's when the little child rests in the arms of the adult who can keep him safe—not from being hurt, but safe in a divine sense. Meaning you are WHOLE and YOU WILL BE OKAY.

It's not about finding the perfect person, Matt. It's about BEING THE PERSON WHO CAN RECOVER, no matter what.

—Meghan Riordan Jarvis, MA, LCSW

Have I mentioned you should get a damn therapist? If you're in a pinch, a therapist friend also works.

As it turns out, Chris's monstrosity of a secret lover was a former client, is married to a woman, and has fourteen children. ☠️ ☠️ ☠️

GOODBYE FOREVER. ✌️

A DREAM CATCHER WORKS, IF YOUR DREAM IS TO BE GAY.

—DEMITRI MARTIN

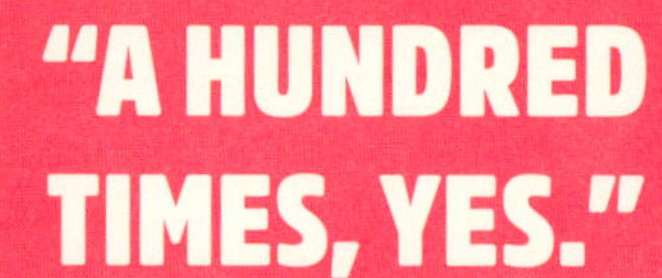
"A HUNDRED
TIMES, YES."
—CHRIS EVANS, AFTER I POPPED
THE QUESTION.

68

Today, I Marry a Man

Growing up, I was hidden behind the illusion of safety—a religious wall that claimed to protect me from a world that was supposedly trying to "steal me away."

Little girls grew up dreaming of the men they'd marry, playing make-believe wedding. They'd find a stray piece of white tulle from their mother's sewing room, fashion a skirt or bridal veil, and march down the aisle toward a make-believe man, confident that one day their dream would become reality.

Because of my upbringing, **daydreaming about walking down the aisle toward a man would've felt ridiculous**. Still, I wish I could go back and dream that dream. Find a piece of black fabric, fashion a bow tie out of it, and march down the aisle toward the man of my dreams.

When I was ten, my older sister had a boyfriend named Joe. Joe was sixteen, nice, and very cute. I remember his soft teenage mustache and smooth arms in a sleeveless shirt. **Even as a young boy, I felt things when I looked at him.**

I never daydreamed about being tossed into the air by Joe or loving him the way a little girl might. If I had known it was possible, maybe I would have. **I did, however, pay close attention to his every move—the way his pants fit, the dirt under his fingernails, his jet-black eyebrows, bright white teeth, and bloodred lips.** I suppose I wanted to marry Joe; I just never knew it was an option.

I came out when I was forty-six. By then, **I'd spent a lifetime pretending to be straight for all the wrong reasons**. You've heard this story before–we all have. Man gets married, raises a family, then comes out decades later to live as a gay man. **To live as himself.** It may sound cliché or dramatic, but every one of these stories is about a boy who went to war with himself at a very early age. On the outside, everything probably seemed fine, but know this: his spirit was a battlefield.

These are stories of survival–not all of us did, ya know? Thank God for those of us who found the strength.

Several years after my long-fought war came to an end, I stumbled upon this beautiful man, and before long, we were shopping for two suits instead of one. Two pairs of black oxfords. Two wedding bands. Two bow ties.

Because we were getting married.

The venue was booked, the guests were invited, and on the day of the wedding, we groomed the hell out of ourselves because, well, you know.

I didn't walk down the aisle simply as a man who decided to be gay and marry another man. **I walked down the aisle carrying in my heart every version of my former self—each one that never got to live honestly.** They all received a personal wedding invitation, and you bet your ass they showed up.

They were:

- The little gay boy who didn't know it was possible to play make-believe wedding with two grooms.
- The innocent ten-year-old who stared at Joe's arms and bloodred lips.
- The high school boy who was so damn lost. So damn gay. So damn sad.
- The college student who kept falling in love with boys who kept falling in love with girls.
- And most importantly, **the one who carried these feelings for all those years**, doing the very best he could to hold it together. The one who survived it all. I am in awe of his strength.

That version—that last one—**he was my best man**.

A week before the wedding, Chris and I picked up our rings. We were supposed to bring them home, put them away, and wait for the wedding officiant to hand them to us during the ceremony. But once we tried them on, we never took them off. **We wanted to be married to each other so badly.**

And now, we are.

'Til death do us part.  

THE QUEER ARE WHO DON'T ANY

ONLY
PEOPLE
THOSE
LOVE
BODY.

—RITA MAE BROWN

69
The Truth About My Soulmate Theory

I hope you've found this bitchy little gay guidebook helpful. And I hope you share it with your gay friends—and your straight friends, too, if you have any.

Before we say goodbye, there's one thing I need to clarify: an amendment to something I mentioned earlier in the gaily devotion called, *"The Soulmate Lie."*

In my theory about soulmates, I said: **Being soulmates is a choice**.

I explained that it's a decision—that we **DECIDE** to be soulmates with someone. I tried to convince you that **there isn't just one person out of nearly eight billion who's specifically designed for you**. I argued that this way of thinking is ridiculous—that our love stories don't need to play out like a Nora Ephron film to be meaningful, special, or forever.

But now, I want to tell you the truth about my soulmate theory.

IT'S BULLSHIT. You heard me. Plain and simple bullshit. 

Why do I say this?

Because of the relationship I have with my husband.

You see (cards on the table), **I actually DO believe Chris is that one person in nearly eight billion**. He's everything to me—every damn thing and more. No other person on this planet could fill his shoes. **He is my all. My life. My love.**

I'm willing to admit I could be wrong—that perhaps our love wasn't created from stardust and sonnets, from answered prayers or the space between two heartbeats.

But isn't this what true love *should* feel like? The belief that no other person on earth could love us so perfectly. That there's no one else we could give ourselves to so wildly and wonderfully.

Chris and I **ARE** soulmates. It's a choice **AND** it's magic. Yes, we chose to be together, though sometimes I wonder if we ever had a choice at all.

THIS is what I wish for you.

Now...

GO FIND YOUR MAN. And once you've found him, **be good enough to KEEP him**.

And please know that—whatever comes your way—there's someone out here cheering for you, rooting for you, **BELIEVING in you**, and wishing you the most meaningful love, you giddy little gay thing.

Because **YOU**, my dear, **are worthy**. **YOU DESERVE IT!**

All the hope in the world, sweetheart. 

And all the love too.

So very sincerely,

Matt Bays

ACKNOWLEDGMENTS

I'd like to thank:

• The Heart-First Collective: LPP, Jessica Kantrowitz, and Kate Mapother. For consistent encouragement and friendship. I love you.

Beth Starr Coryell, for *always* encouraging me to achieve more with my life. I can't think of a single endeavor I've pursued that you haven't embraced with excitement and your full support.

Laura Parrott Perry—my first call. For always being honest, even when it hurts. There's not enough room in these pages. Our friendship is forever. Can't wait to get matching facelifts when we're no longer this gorgeous.

Julie Lange, for sharing your bestie with me, and for long-ass FaceTimes about everything that no one has ever cared about...except us. Have you even watched *One True Thing* yet? God.

Ingrid Beck, for your belief in my writing, and for your support and guidance throughout this journey. That late night Cambodian Zoom call turned into something amazing.

Ariel Curry, for seeing the potential in this book. And for the gift of your powerful editing skills. Being a part of Sourcebooks is a dream come true. Love to you, Dominique, and the whole team who made this book so stunning.

Matt Heincker, my podcast partner and friend, for being on this journey with me, and for your no-nonsense wisdom. I love you, Matty. Very much. Continue living in rivers of self-love, my friend. And let's find these boys a man!

The miraculous Ty Wyss, for being a haven for my good, best Judy. Also, remember that day at the little bistro when we decided not to talk about the tough stuff? Well, you made it out, too, honey...and just look at you now.

My Chloe, honey-baby, sugar-pie. At least three times a week you FaceTime your dad. Every single time I see your sweet face on my screen, I feel so damn lucky. You made me a dad, and I adore you. The level of compassion you live your life with makes me so proud, sweetie. I love you. Always.

The boys in the LGBTQ+ community. You've given me quite the education, for which I am truly grateful. I'll always be hoping and helping you find the man of your dreams. Trust and believe that you deserve an explosive and expansive love. Look for it. Work for it. Wait for it. Expect it.

I would also like to thank Aiden, Connor, Carol, Matt and Heather Evans, Brian Edwards, Julie Gallutia, Julie Hanser, Kristin Watson Heintz, Steve and Angie Kissing, Tracy Manning, Ryan Poe, Leslie Robbins, Tab Sabin, Alyssa Sulzener, Barb and Jason Thorp, Katrina Hodge Willis, and my perfect, sweet, kind, and gentle momma. What would I do without you? I have such amazing friends and family.

And last, to my husband and best friend—the *real* Chris Evans. I found you on my fiftieth birthday. I'm keeping you forever. You've *made* my life, do you realize that? You are the perfect man—for me. I love you times infinity. And guess what? We *still* get to do this! Isn't it stupid? What if they find out? Shouldn't we be in jail for having this much fun? 🚔 🚨 👮 ⛓️ We're the luckiest!

NOTES

THE SOULMATE LIE

1 "About Tinder," Tinder Newsroom, accessed April 7, 2025, https://www.tinderpressroom.com/about.

THE AGING QUEEN

1 "*Mommy Dearest* Quotes," IMDB, accessed April 3, 2025, https://www.imdb.com/title/tt0082766/quotes/.

2 *Will & Grace*, season 5, episode 14, "Fagmalion Part 2: Attack of the Clones," written by David Kohan, Max Mutchnick, Gary Janetti, directed by James Burrows, aired January 30, 2003, on NBC.

THE STABLE GAY

1 Laura Parrott Perry, conversation with author. (I wish this phrase was mine.)

THE ASSHOLE ADJUSTMENT

1 "RuPaul's Sissy That Walk Official Music Video," posted May 12, 2014, by WOW Presents, YouTube, https://www.youtube.com/watch?v=M4d20Tyzlv0.

2 Horacio Jones, *I Am the Love of My Life* (CreateSpace, 2016).

GET OFF GRINDR

1 Suzannah Weiss, "6 Surprising Beauty Benefits of Orgasming," *Glamour*, December 30, 2016, https://www.glamour.com/story/beauty-benefits-of-orgasm.

2 Marie Kondo, *The Life-Changing Magic of Tidying Up: The Japanese Art of Decluttering and Organizing* (Ten Speed Press, 2014).

THE AGE GAP TRAP

1 Annabel Fenwick Elliott, "'He Never Says I Love You Back...The Insecurity Eats Me Alive': From No-Strings Sex to Feeling Judged, Cougars Reveal What It's REALLY Like to Date Younger Men," *Daily Mail*, updated June 16, 2015, https://www.dailymail.co.uk/femail/article-3118413/He-never-says-love-insecurity-eats-alive-no-strings-sex-feeling-judged-cougars-reveal-s-REALLY-like-date-younger-men.html.

DICK PICS

1 Michele Meleen, "40 Gay Love Quotes That Celebrate the Power of Connection," LoveToKnow, updated June 6, 2024, https://www.lovetoknow.com/quotes-quips/love/gay-love-quotes.

RED FLAGS & GREEN LIGHTS

1 "Love Story or LIFE Story? Esther Perel," posted November 8, 2022, by lovelife8302, YouTube, https://www.youtube.com/shorts/2yoqDSI8NxU.

GOD, GAY...GOOD LORD!

1 "How Religious Are Americans?" Gallup, March 29, 2024, https://news.gallup.com/poll/358364/religious-americans.aspx.

2 "A Survey of LGBT Americans: Chapter 6: Religion," Pew Research Center, June 13, 2013, https://www.pewresearch.org/social-trends/2013/06/13/chapter-6-religion/.

3 RuPaul Charles (@RuPaul), "If you can't love yourself, how in the hell you gonna love somebody else?" Twitter (now X), June 12, 2017, https://x.com/RuPaul/status/874306994626109440?lang=en.

FEAR—PART 2

1 "My 'fear' is my substance, and probably the best part of me," Goodreads, accessed April 3, 2025, https://www.goodreads.com/quotes/357470-my-fear-is-my-substance-and-probably-the-best-part.

2 Nicole Sobon, *Program 13 (The Emile Reed Chronicles)* (CreateSpace, 2011).

BREAKING UP 💔

1 "The most terrible thing about it is not that it breaks one's heart—hearts are made to be broken—but that it turns one's heart to stone," Goodreads, accessed April 3, 2025, https://www.goodreads.com/quotes/194189-the-most-terrible-thing-about-it-is-not-that-it.

GRADUATION & LETTING GO

1 Paulo Coelho, *The Alchemist* (HarperCollins, 1993).

HOW TO KEEP A GAY MAN

1 "It takes courage to grow up and become who you really are," BrainyQuote, accessed April 3, 2025, https://www.brainyquote.com/quotes/e_e_cummings_161593.

STOP DOING PORN

1 Gary Gilles, "How Porn Affects Relationships," MentalHealth.com, January 20, 2025, https://www.mentalhealth.com/blog/how-pornography-distorts-intimate-relationships.

LET'S GET VULNERABLE

1 Brené Brown, *Daring Greatly: How the Courage to Be Vulnerable Transforms the Way We Live, Love, Parent, and Lead* (Avery, 2012), 2.

"WE'RE IN AN OPEN RELATIONSHIP"

1 Katie Couric Media, "Here's Why You Might Want to Try an Open Relationship," Katie Couric, November 22, 2022, https://katiecouric.com/lifestyle/relationships/what-is-an-open-relationship/.

2 Moshe Ratson, "Are You Open to an Open Relationship?," *Psychology Today*, accessed April 7, 2025, https://www.psychologytoday.com/us/blog/the-wisdom-of-anger/202409/are-you-open-to-an-open-relationship.

3 Brené Brown, *The Gifts of Imperfection: Let Go of Who You Think You're Supposed to Be and Embrace Who You Are* (Hazelden, 2010), 12.

BE WILLING TO BE WRONG

1 "Top 200 Jane Fonda Quotes (2025 Update)," QuoteFancy, accessed April 3, 2025, https://quotefancy.com/jane-fonda-quotes/page/2.

SUBSTANCE ABUSE

1 "Why Do Gay Men Sometimes Struggle with Substance Abuse?" American Addiction Centers, updated November 22, 2024, https://americanaddictioncenters.org/lgbtqiapk-addiction/gay.

2 Search results for "penis definition," Google, https://www.google.com/search?q=penis+definition

CHANGE IT UP

1 Kendra Cherry, "What It Means If You're Bored in a Relationship," Verywell Mind, updated February 10, 2025, https://www.verywellmind.com/signs-of-a-boring-relationship-and-what-to-do-about-it-5206299.

MORE THAN YOU COULD EVER ASK FOR OR IMAGINE

1 "In the Meantime" by Jessica Ray, track 4 on Jessica Ray, *Sentimental Creatures*, 2015.

HOT MESS CLINGY & THE PUSH-AWAY PARTNER

1 Sanjana Gupta, "What Does Secure Attachment Look and Feel Like? Plus How to Develop It," Verywell Mind, updated April 18, 2024, https://www.verywellmind.com/secure-attachment-signs-benefits-and-how-to-cultivate-it-8628802.

CODEPENDENCE

1 "Codependency," *Psychology Today*, accessed April 7, 2025, https://www.psychologytoday.com/us/basics/codependency.

2 Melody Beattie, *Codependent No More: How to Stop Controlling Others and Start Caring for Yourself* (Spiegel & Grau, 2022).

BORED MAN SEEKS PERSONAL GROWTH

1 Gia Miller, "The Benefits of Boredom," Child Mind Institute, November 13, 2024, https://childmind.org/article/the-benefits-of-boredom/.

LIKE A PRAYER

1 "Giving Thanks Can Make You Happier," Harvard Health Publishing, August 14, 2021, https://www.health.harvard.edu/healthbeat/giving-thanks-can-make-you-happier.

ABOUT THE AUTHOR

PHOTO BY TRACIE JEAN PHOTO

MATT BAYS is a speaker, life coach, and author celebrated for his nationally released memoir, *Finding God in the Ruins*, and debut LGBTQ memoir, *Leather & Lace*. His writing and music have been featured in *HuffPost*, the *New York Times*, the *Advocate*, and *Out Magazine.* With a compelling podcast, *How to Find (& Keep) a Gay Man*, Matt extends his passion by empowering gay men who desire connection. He joins the ranks of writers such as Anne Lamott and Glennon Doyle in offering readers honest, raw, funny, and insightful compassion for the journey of life. Once a closeted minister, Matt's unique perspective inspires authenticity and courage. Matt lives in Porto, Portugal, with his husband, Chris. You can connect with him on Instagram @mattbayswriter.